Machine Learning Models of Handwritten Character Recognition

JT Savage

TABLE OF CONTENTS

CHAPTER - 1

INTRODUCTION

In today's world, computers significantly impact our lives, and we handle nearly all essential tasks electronically. Given the extensive use of computers, it is crucial to develop efficient, user-friendly, and rapid methods for data transfer between humans and computers. Document Analysis and Recognition (DAR) systems play a critical role in enabling this data exchange. A key component of DAR systems is Optical Character Recognition (OCR), which allows for the recognition of both printed and handwritten text. Handwritten text recognition systems are especially valuable, providing a seamless interface that enhances communication between users and computers, enabling machines to interpret and process handwritten documents [1]. Such systems contribute substantially to bridging the gap between humans and machines [2].

Although considerable research has focused on recognizing characters in Indian scripts, the challenge of efficient data exchange between humans and machines remains unresolved for these scripts. This thesis addresses these challenges by developing a framework for predicting age, gender, and handedness in handwritten character recognition of the Gurumukhi script, which is used for the Punjabi language, one of India's official languages. Notably, Gurumukhi is the tenth most widely used script globally [3].

1.1 Importance of Handwriting as a Biometric Trait

Handwriting is highly individualized, varying greatly from person to person. Unlike facial recognition or fingerprints, handwriting captures dynamic aspects that reflect the writer's cognitive state, neuromuscular processes, and learned writing style. This individuality makes it an effective biometric trait, capable of revealing information about the writer's age, gender, and even handedness, or dominant hand.

In handwriting, specific characteristics such as stroke pressure, slant, letter size, and spacing are not only influenced by training and practice but also shaped by one's physical and psychological traits. For instance, younger writers may exhibit faster, looser strokes compared to older adults, who might show more deliberate, controlled movements. Similarly, gender differences are often reflected in stylistic variations, with some studies suggesting that males may write with more angular and larger letters, while females tend to use rounded and smaller

letters. Handedness introduces additional distinctions, as left-handed and right-handed individuals approach letter formation and slanting differently.
Handwriting-based biometrics present distinct advantages, particularly in applications where capturing other biometric traits is either impractical or challenging. For example, in forensic investigations or historical document analysis, where only handwritten samples are available, handwriting analysis can help infer demographic characteristics, aiding in profiling or identity verification. This research, focusing on age, gender, and handedness prediction from Gurumukhi script seeks to deepen understanding in this domain and expand the scope of handwriting-based biometrics.

1.2 Overview of the Gurumukhi Script

Gurumukhi is the script used to write Punjabi, a prominent language spoken by millions, primarily in the Indian state of Punjab and by the global Punjabi diaspora. The word "Gurumukhi" translates to "from the mouth of the Guru," reflecting its deep roots in Sikh history and culture [3]. It was standardized by Guru Angad Dev Ji, the second Guru of Sikhism, in the 16th century, making it a script with rich cultural and historical significance. The Gurumukhi script is not only central to the Punjabi language but also holds a sacred position in Sikhism, as it is the script in which the Guru Granth Sahib, the holy book of Sikhs, is written.

Structurally, Gurumukhi is an abugida script, meaning that each consonant carries an inherent vowel sound that can be modified or omitted through diacritical marks. It comprises 35 primary letters, including consonants, vowels and additional modifiers that represent unique phonetic sounds not commonly found in Latin-based scripts. Gurumukhi writing follows a linear structure from left to right and is characterized by a distinctive horizontal line connecting the tops of characters within a word, known as the "head stroke."

Due to these unique characteristics, recognizing Gurumukhi text, especially in handwritten form, poses distinct challenges in the fields of document analysis and OCR. The variability in handwriting styles, the presence of diacritics, and the combination of complex shapes make Gurumukhi character recognition a complex task. Although Gurmukhi ranks as the tenth most used script worldwide, it has received disproportionately limited research attention compared to other global scripts especially in the field of handwriting recognition systems [3]. Figure 1.1 depicts the components used in the Gurumukhi script character set for collecting datasets.

Consonants	ੳ	ਅ	ੲ	ਸ	ਹ	ਕ	ਖ	ਗ	ਘ	ਙ	
	ਚ	ਛ	ਜ	ਝ	ਞ	ਟ	ਠ	ਡ	ਢ	ਣ	
	ਤ	ਥ	ਦ	ਧ	ਨ	ਪ	ਫ	ਬ	ਭ	ਮ	
	ਯ	ਰ	ਲ	ਵ	ੜ	ਸ਼	ਖ਼	ਗ਼	ਜ਼	ਫ਼	ਲ਼
Vowel Modifiers	◌ਾ	ਿ◌	◌ੀ	◌ੁ	◌ੂ	◌ੇ	◌ੈ	◌ੋ	◌ੌ		
Nasal Symbols	◌ੰ	◌ਂ	*addak* Symbol	◌ੱ							

Figure 1.1: Components in Gurumukhi script

1.2.1 Importance of Gurumukhi Handwriting Recognition

Developing a robust system for recognizing handwritten Gurumukhi script holds substantial cultural, practical, and academic significance. As the primary medium for both modern communication and sacred texts in Punjabi culture, the Gurumukhi script represents a vital component of linguistic and cultural identity. An accurate handwriting recognition system for Gurumukhi has the potential to support various applications, from preserving historical documents to enhancing human-computer interaction for Punjabi speakers [3].

In the digital age, such a system could serve a wide range of practical purposes, including archiving handwritten documents, enabling easier access to historical texts, and allowing for more inclusive and efficient digital interactions for native Punjabi speakers [25]. By developing a recognition system specifically tailored to Gurumukhi script, this research aims to address the current gap in document analysis for Indian scripts and to contribute to the broader field of multilingual OCR.

1.3 Handwritten Character Recognition (HCR)

Handwritten Character Recognition (HCR) is the process of automatically interpreting human handwriting using computer systems. Based on how the handwriting data is captured, HCR can be divided into two main types: offline and online recognition as shown in Figures 1.2 (a) and (b), respectively. Both types have unique characteristics, advantages, and challenges especially when applied to complex scripts like Gurumukhi.

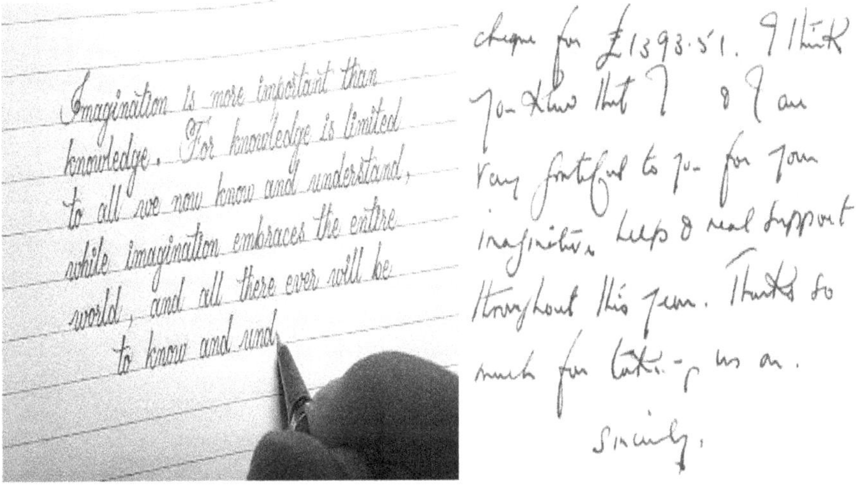

(a) (b)

Figure 1.2: (a) offline handwriting (b) online handwriting

1.3.1 Offline Handwritten Character Recognition

Offline handwritten character recognition is the process of recognizing handwriting from static images, such as scanned documents, photographs, or previously written text on paper. In this approach, the computer system interprets handwriting based on a two-dimensional image of the final written product, without access to dynamic information like stroke order, speed, or pen pressure.

Key Characteristics of Offline HCR

- **Static Image Processing:** Offline HCR works with an image of handwriting, where each character and word must be interpreted solely based on its appearance.

- **No Dynamic Information:** Offline systems lack details such as stroke direction, speed, and pressure, which are valuable for distinguishing ambiguous characters.
- **Challenging Pre-processing Requirements:** To improve recognition accuracy, offline systems often perform pre-processing tasks such as binarization, noise removal, and skew correction. These steps help in reducing image artifacts and enhancing the clarity of characters.

Challenges of Offline HCR for Gurumukhi Script

- **Head Strokes:** Gurumukhi characters are often connected by a head stroke, which can vary in continuity and intensity in handwritten samples. Segmenting characters from this head stroke without losing critical character details is challenging.
- **Diverse Writing Styles:** Handwriting varies significantly between individuals, particularly in scripts like Gurumukhi where characters have intricate shapes. These variations can make it difficult for the system to differentiate similar characters.
- **Complex Character Structure:** Gurumukhi characters often include diacritical marks, which can be inconsistently placed in handwriting. This variability in diacritic location and appearance can affect the system's ability to recognize characters accurately.

Approaches to Offline HCR for Gurumukhi Script

Offline HCR for Gurumukhi script typically involves feature extraction and machine learning techniques to classify characters based on their shape and structure. Techniques include:

- **Convolutional Neural Networks (CNNs):** CNNs are commonly used for offline HCR as they are effective in learning spatial features from images. For Gurumukhi, CNNs can capture complex character details and improve recognition rates despite variations in handwriting styles.
- **Support Vector Machines (SVMs):** SVMs are often used in combination with feature extraction methods to classify Gurumukhi characters based on their structural features.
- **Hidden Markov Models (HMMs):** HMMs are also used in offline HCR for sequential data modelling particularly when recognizing text written in a cursive style.

1.3.2 Online Handwritten Character Recognition

Online handwritten character recognition involves real-time recognition of handwriting captured as it is written, typically using electronic devices like digital tablets or smartphones. This method uses dynamic data, including the sequence of strokes, speed, and pressure, to interpret characters, providing a richer dataset for accurate recognition [4].

Key Characteristics of Online HCR

- **Real-Time Data Capture:** Online systems record handwriting dynamically, capturing the sequence and direction of strokes, pen pressure, and even speed of writing.
- **Rich Stroke Information:** The sequence in which characters are written can help in distinguishing between similar shapes, as the system has access to each individual stroke.
- **Instant Recognition and Feedback:** Online systems can provide instant feedback, which is useful in applications such as educational tools and interactive interfaces.

Advantages of Online HCR for Gurumukhi Script

- **Improved Character Differentiation:** Gurumukhi script includes several visually similar characters that can be hard to distinguish in a static image. The availability of stroke sequence information in online HCR makes it easier to differentiate between these characters [5].
- **Enhanced Recognition of Diacritics:** Online systems can better handle diacritics in Gurumukhi characters by capturing the order and position of each stroke, which helps accurately associate diacritics with their base characters.
- **Increased Accuracy in Complex Characters:** Gurumukhi characters, which can include multiple components or diacritical marks, benefit from the additional detail in stroke data, leading to higher recognition accuracy [6].

Approaches to Online HCR for Gurumukhi Script

Online HCR for Gurumukhi utilizes algorithms that consider both the spatial and temporal aspects of handwritten input. Common approaches include [7]:

- **Recurrent Neural Networks (RNNs):** RNNs are effective in processing sequential data, making them suitable for online HCR as they can model the sequence of pen strokes in Gurumukhi characters.
- **Long Short-Term Memory (LSTM) Networks:** LSTMs are a type of RNN specifically designed to handle longer sequences, such as complex Gurumukhi characters written in multiple strokes. LSTMs help in preserving relevant stroke information over time, enhancing recognition.
- **Dynamic Time Warping (DTW):** DTW is used to align two sequences of handwriting, making it useful for comparing stroke patterns. This technique allows the system to match the input sequence with pre-stored templates, accommodating variations in writing speed and size.

Table 1.1 shows the comparison of offline and online HCR Systems, the key differences between offline and online handwritten character recognition systems are highlighted [8]. The table provides a comparison based on aspects such as data input type, availability of stroke information, applicability, recognition challenges, and specific implications for recognizing Gurumukhi script.

Table 1.1: Comparison of offline and online Handwritten Character Recognition (HCR) systems

Aspect	Offline HCR	Online HCR
Data Input	Static image (e.g., scanned text)	Real-time stroke data (e.g., tablet or stylus)
Stroke Information	No access to dynamic stroke data	Captures stroke order, direction, speed, and pressure
Applicability	Ideal for digitizing existing handwritten documents	Useful in real-time applications, interactive systems
Recognition Challenges	Requires pre-processing to improve accuracy	More accurate with detailed stroke information
Application in Gurumukhi	Complex due to diverse handwriting styles and head strokes	More reliable for complex characters with diacritics

Most research on optical character recognition of Indian scripts has focused on printed characters, while relatively few studies address the recognition of handwritten characters. Existing studies primarily cover scripts such as Bangla, Devanagari, and Kannada. Notably, foundational work in these scripts was conducted by Pal and Chaudhuri for Bangla [9], Bansal and Sinha for Devanagari [10], and Ashwin and Sastry for Kannada [11]. The work presented in this thesis aims to advance the recognition of offline handwritten Gurumukhi script, contributing to the development of recognition systems that could be extended to other Indian scripts with structural similarities to Gurumukhi.

Recognition of offline handwritten documents remains an active research area in pattern recognition. Over recent years, various research facilities globally have invested in handwriting recognition studies. Cursive handwriting recognition is challenging due to significant shape variations and character overlaps. In an offline handwriting recognition system, pre-written documents are scanned into digital images. Such documents contain considerable variability in writing styles, character sizes, and other attributes [12].

Handwritten documents are ubiquitous in locations such as post offices, banks, insurance offices, and educational institutions, where substantial handwritten data is generated through forms, postal addresses, signatures, and more. In such contexts, the proposed research would be highly valuable in advancing handwritten document recognition [13-15].

This research outlines the design of a system to convert offline handwritten Gurumukhi script documents into a machine-readable format. This system offers a promising approach to enhance the interface between humans and computers, making handwritten Gurumukhi script documents accessible for digital processing.

1.4 Age, Gender and Handedness Prediction

Age, gender and handedness Identification of handwritten text is a type of biometric recognition where one can identify the writer's age, gender, and handedness based on his/her handwriting. This concept merges the fields of biometric authentication and behavioural pattern recognition, offering valuable insights into how certain physical and psychological traits manifest in a person's writing.

1.4.1 Age Classification

The age classification system classifies the age of a person by dividing it into various classes based on the handwriting of the individual. This process involves analysing the distinct features that change with age, such as handwriting pressure, stroke formation, consistency, slant, and spacing between characters. These features evolve due to physiological, psychological and motor skill development as individuals grow [16].

For example, age in the range of 5-10 is a single class; 11-15 is another class, and so on. The prediction of human age based on various techniques is very similar now, so there is a great need to develop a novel application based on it. These groups reflect distinct stages in the development of motor and cognitive skills, each of which influences handwriting characteristics differently. By analysing these features, a machine learning model can predict the age group of an individual based on their handwriting.

Figures 1.3 a, b shows handwriting samples in Gurumukhi script from an 8-year-old and a 15-year-old child.

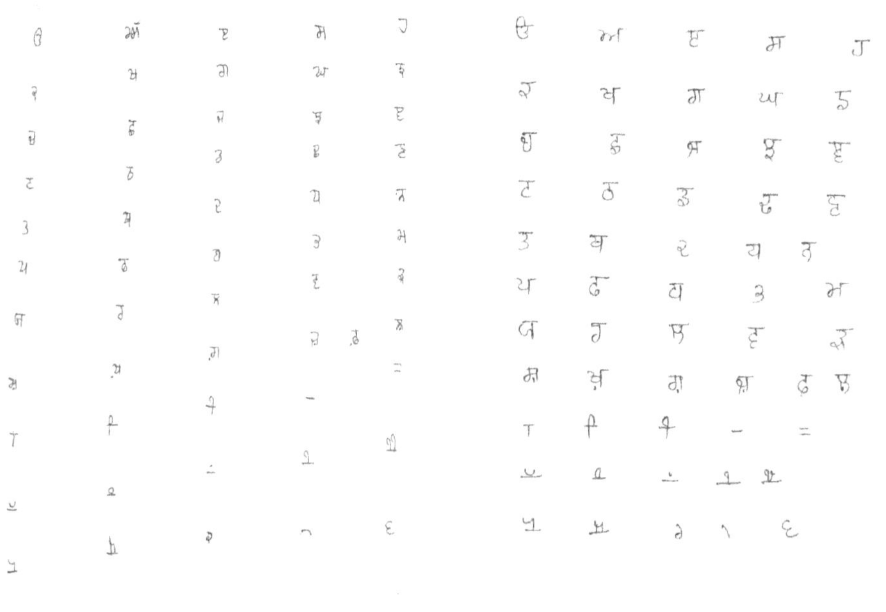

(a) (b)

Figure 1.3 Handwriting samples of 8 years (a) and 15 years old (b) in Gurumukhi script

1.4.2 Gender Classification

Gender is a criticality and its classification is a two-class problem that classifies males and females based on biometric traits such as handwriting, facial expressions, speech, etc. [17-18]. Table 1.2 depicts various characteristics of male and female handwriting. Gender classification is necessary because separating the population into sub-categories is an interesting fact to study and is important for the development of many applications [19]. Based on the features extracted from the human body, such as facial expressions, behaviour, etc., various approaches are already available for gender classification. The difference between male and female handwriting can also be noticed from the visual appearance of the handwriting. Figure 1.4 & 1.5 shows different samples of male and female handwriting [20].

Table 1.2: Characteristics of male and female handwriting

Male Handwriting	Female Handwriting
Small	Neater and Tidier
Unorganized	Organized
Rushed	Bigger
More italic	Regular
Messier	More Rounded
More angular	Curvier
More Scribbling	Bubbly

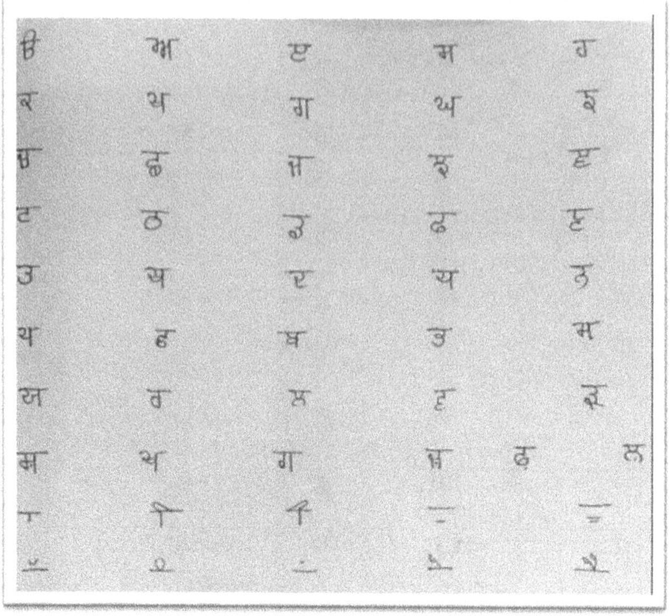

Figure 1.4: A few samples of Gurumukhi character set by male writer

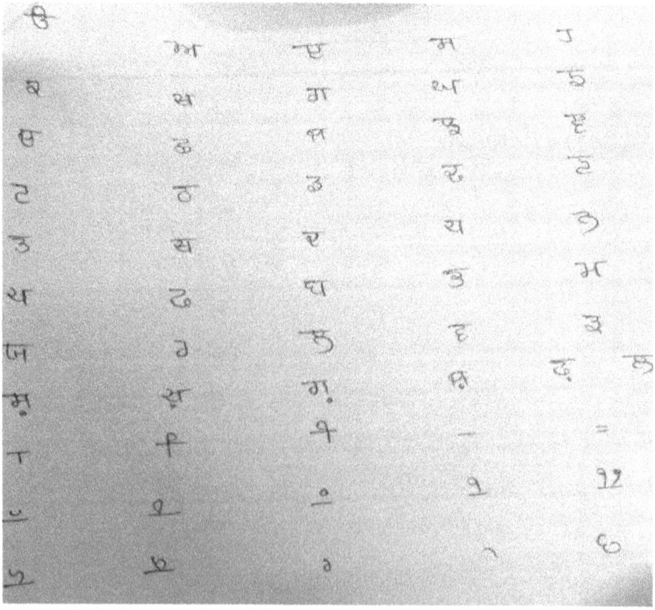

Figure 1.5: A few samples of Gurumukhi character set by female writer

1.4.3 Handedness Prediction

Handedness prediction is an important task in the field of pattern recognition, where the goal is to classify individuals as either "right-handed" or "left-handed." This is a binary classification problem like many real-world classification tasks; handedness prediction faces challenges related to class imbalance. Specifically, the available datasets for handedness prediction typically exhibit an unequal distribution between the two subclasses with a predominance of right-handed individuals [21].

In most publicly available datasets, around 90% of the samples correspond to right-handed individuals, while only about 10% represent left-handed individuals. This imbalance is reflective of the global proportion of right- and left-handed people, where roughly 90% of the population is right-handed and 10% is left-handed. The disproportionate representation of right-handed individuals in the datasets often leads to difficulties in training accurate predictive models. This is because machine learning algorithms, especially those that rely on statistical patterns from the data, tend to be biased toward the majority class [22]. As a result, the model may become overly sensitive to right-handed characteristics, while failing to accurately recognize the more limited patterns associated with left-handedness.

The challenge of class imbalance in handedness prediction is similar to other fields where datasets exhibit unequal class distributions. For instance, in medical diagnoses where certain diseases are less common than others, or in fraud detection, where fraudulent cases are far fewer than legitimate transactions. To mitigate these challenges, techniques such as resampling, synthetic data generation, or adjusting the decision threshold can be used to achieve more balanced prediction performance across both classes.

The phases of feature extraction, classification, and prediction are required for developing a framework for age, gender, and handedness prediction, as shown in Figure 1.6.

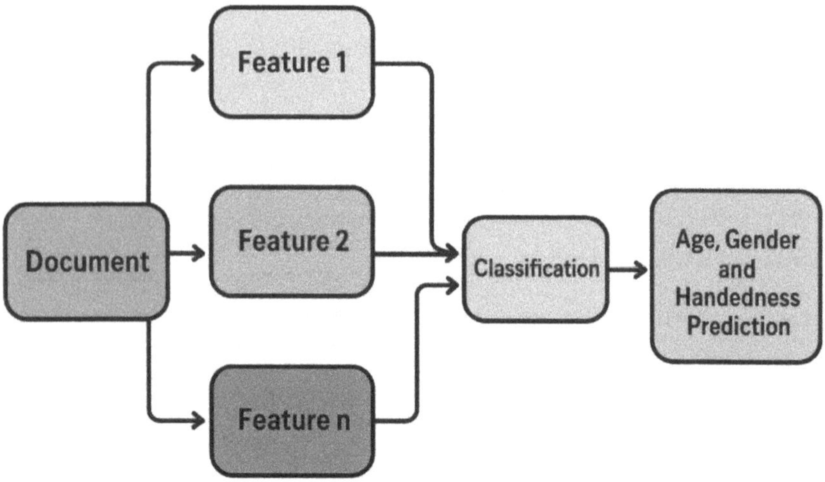

Figure 1.6: Age, gender and handedness classification process

1.5 Application Areas

There are numerous applications and benefits of this novel method in the pattern recognition system. These systems are adopted in a variety of civilian applications for enhancing security and privacy [23-26]. Various application areas of age, gender, and handedness prediction systems are depicted in Table 1.3 [27].

Table 1.3. Applications of age, gender and handedness prediction from handwritten text

Prediction	Applications
Age	- Security and video surveillance
	- Electronic customer relationship management
	- Biometrics
	- Electronic vending machines
	- Human-computer interaction
	- Entertainment
	- Cosmetology
	- Forensic art
	- Crime investigation
	- Criminal justice system
	- Forensic linguists for evidence analysis

Gender	- Verifying emails
	- Specific category of suspects
Handedness	- Forensic biometrics
	- Authenticity of documents in court of law
	- Authentication of financial transactions
	- Signature verification
	- Resolving suspects

1.6 Stages of an offline HCR System

1.6.1 Digitization Process

For the digitization phase, the data is first converted into digital format and organized into bit form. Offline data should be scanned at 300 dots per inch that is considered as the standard value. In the scanning process, the original image is converted into a digital image, which is then taken as an input to the pre-processing phase. The target of performing digitization is to abridge the dependency on the original paper with no effect on the efficiency and the security [28].

1.6.2 Pre-processing

This phase deals with cleaning and normalizing the scanned documents. It covers the normalization of the grey-level character images into a window. Normalization results in the generation of the bitmap image which is converted into the thinned image using a parallel thinning algorithm. The pre-processing process affects the feature extraction process required for the classification. It is the initial stage of the word recognition system [29].

1.6.3 Feature Extraction

This is the main phase in handwriting recognition and in machine learning and computer vision problems. The characterization of the features helps in distinguishing the age and gender of the writer. The goal of this phase is to extract different features based on the pre-segmented character image. This phase produces the pertinent information about the character or the word present in the handwriting or an entity e.g., character, word or document which are the inputs for the classification phase with less time, complexity, and computation [30]. There are following two categories of features called geometrical features and transformed features:

- Geometrical features take the geometrical information of the given handwritten images e.g., slant, roundness, orientation, curvatures, etc. Geometrical features can be extracted directly from the data images and can be constructed with the help of geometrical elements like curves, lines, points, or surfaces. The feature value shows the pattern and styles of handwritten images [31].
- Transformed features can be received because of mathematical transformation applied on the given handwritten data images i.e., Gabor features, Fourier features, WDLBP features [32].

1.6.4 Classification

This part is a decision-making part, which performs the classification of the given character, word, or entity with the training database by using various parametric and nonparametric classifiers that come under the category of statistical classifiers. It is better to employ hybrid classifiers to increase the identification accuracy rate [33]. In this step, the features previously presented are used to decide which category handwriting belongs to. When performing the classification, each element of the feature vectors will be used as a separate input for the classifier.

1.7 Objectives of this Work

The objectives of the proposed study are outlined as follows:

1. To analyse the existing techniques for age, gender, and handedness prediction from offline handwritten test.
2. To generate a corpus of Gurumukhi handwritten character set and to preprocess the dataset.
3. To propose an efficient feature extraction technique for age, gender and handedness prediction based on the offline handwritten Gurumukhi text.
4. To improve the efficiency of classification using hybridization of different classifiers.
5. Development of a technique for age, gender, and handedness prediction from offline handedness prediction from offline handwritten Gurumukhi text.
6. To test and validate the performance of proposed technique using various performance parameters.

1.8 Assumptions

The following assumptions and constraints were considered while conducting the experiments in this thesis:

i. **Document Resolution**: All handwritten documents were scanned at a resolution of 300 dpi to ensure sufficient detail for feature extraction and analysis.

ii. **Noise-Free Data**: The handwritten text samples used in this study were pre-processed to be free from noise, eliminating the need for additional noise removal techniques. Skew detection and correction were also deemed unnecessary as the input text was uniformly aligned [34].

iii. **Text-Only Content**: The dataset exclusively consists of handwritten textual data, with no inclusion of non-textual elements such as images, figures, or symbols, ensuring a focused analysis on handwritten characters.

iv. **Uniform Script**: All handwriting samples belong to the Gurumukhi script, without any multilingual content or mixing of other scripts, maintaining consistency in script-specific feature extraction.

v. **Controlled Writing Environment**: Participants were instructed to write under standardized conditions, such as using similar writing instruments and paper types, to reduce variations introduced by external factors.

vi. **No Overlapping Characters**: The handwritten text samples were curated to avoid overlapping or excessively connected characters, simplifying the recognition process.

1.9 Major Contributions and Achievements

i. **Analysis of Existing Techniques for Age, Gender, and Handedness Prediction** A comprehensive review and analysis of existing techniques for predicting age, gender, and handedness from handwritten text were conducted. This analysis identified key gaps and limitations in the current approaches particularly for Indic scripts like Gurumukhi. The findings highlighted the need for a dedicated system to address these challenges and provided the foundational knowledge for the development of a more efficient solution.

ii. **Generation of a Corpus of Gurumukhi Handwritten Character Set and Dataset Pre-processing**

A significant achievement of this research was the creation of a large and diverse corpus of Gurumukhi handwritten characters. The dataset consists of 74,760 handwritten Gurumukhi characters contributed by 267 participants ensuring a balanced representation of both genders and varying age groups. The pre-processing of this dataset included noise removal, normalization, and the standardization of handwriting samples, which were scanned at 300 dpi to ensure high-quality input for further analysis. This corpus serves as a valuable resource for future research in handwriting recognition and attribute prediction for the Gurumukhi script.

iii. **Proposed Efficient Feature Extraction Technique for Age, Gender, and Handedness Prediction**

A novel and efficient feature extraction technique was developed specifically for the Gurumukhi script focusing on key geometric features such as stroke density, slant, and curvature of handwritten characters. These features were found to be critical for distinguishing between different age groups, genders, and handedness in handwriting. This method significantly improves the accuracy and robustness of handwriting-based prediction systems by focusing on unique characteristics of the Gurumukhi script.

iv. **Improvement in Classification Efficiency through Hybridization of Classifiers**

One of the major innovations in this work was the hybridization of multiple classification algorithms to improve prediction accuracy. The research combined various machine learning models including Support Vector Machines (SVM), Random Forests, K-nearest neighbour's, Multilayer perceptron's, and Neural Networks, to create a robust classification framework for age, gender, and handedness prediction. The hybrid approach effectively leveraged the strengths of each classifier, thereby enhancing the overall performance of the system especially in handling the complexities of handwritten Gurumukhi text.

v. **Development of a Technique for Age, Gender, and Handedness Prediction from Offline Handwritten Gurumukhi Text**

The core achievement of this thesis was the development of an effective system for predicting age, gender, and handedness based on offline handwritten Gurumukhi text. This system uses a holistic recognition approach treating each handwritten character as a whole entity rather than segmenting it into individual components. By overcoming the segmentation challenges inherent in Gurumukhi script, the system offers high accuracy in predicting these attributes from handwritten text. This work provides a breakthrough in handwriting recognition for Indic scripts with a particular focus on Punjabi.

vi. **Testing and Validation of the Proposed Technique Using Various Performance Parameters**

The performance of the proposed technique was rigorously tested and validated using a variety of performance metrics, including precision, recall, F1- Score, and accuracy. Extensive testing demonstrated the robustness of the system, with results indicating significant improvement over existing methods in the prediction of age, gender, and handedness from handwritten Gurumukhi text. The validation phase further ensured the generalizability and applicability of the system in real-world scenarios, confirming its potential for deployment in domains such as forensics, education, and healthcare.

1.10 Organization of Thesis

The main objective of this thesis is to develop an offline handwritten Gurumukhi script recognition system. We have recognized offline handwritten Gurumukhi characters with different recognition methods. We have also implemented a handwriting grading system based on offline Gurumukhi characters. The organization of the thesis is briefly outlined as below.

Chapter 1: Introduction

This chapter introduces the research problem, the significance of handwriting analysis for demographic prediction, and the objectives of the study. It also outlines the contributions of the research and provides an overview of the thesis structure.

Chapter 2: Review of Literature

This chapter presents a comprehensive review of existing literature on handwriting recognition, demographic prediction from handwritten text, and the application of machine learning and deep learning techniques for similar tasks. It highlights the gaps in current research that this study aims to address.

Chapter 3: Phases of Handwritten Character Recognition & Evaluation Metrics

This chapter discusses the various stages involved in handwritten character recognition, including data collection, pre-processing, feature extraction, classification, and evaluation. It also elaborates on the evaluation metrics used to assess the performance of the proposed models.

Chapter 4: Proposed Methodology for Age, Gender & Handedness Prediction Using CNN

This chapter outlines the methodology for predicting age, gender, and handedness from handwritten Gurumukhi characters using Convolutional Neural Networks (CNNs). The architecture, design decisions, and model parameters are described in detail.

Chapter 5: Proposed Method for Gender Classification Using Hybridized Feature Extraction and Multiple Classifiers

This chapter focuses on the hybrid approach for gender classification, combining feature extraction techniques with multiple classifiers such as Support Vector Machines (SVM), K-Nearest Neighbours (KNN), and Random Forest. The proposed method is explained and its implementation details are provided.

Chapter 6: Proposed Method for Age Classification and Handedness Prediction Using Machine Learning Models

This chapter presents the machine learning-based methods for age classification and handedness prediction. It discusses the models used, including Multi-Layer Perceptron (MLP) and Support Vector Machines (SVM), and outlines the feature engineering and pre-processing techniques applied.

Chapter 7: Results and Discussion

This chapter presents the results of the experiments conducted on the proposed methodologies. The performance of the models for age, gender, and handedness prediction is discussed, along with a detailed analysis of the findings and implications.

Chapter 8: Challenges and Limitations in Handwriting-Based Demographic Prediction

This chapter addresses the challenges and limitations encountered during the research, including issues related to dataset quality, feature extraction, model performance, and generalization. Suggestions for overcoming these challenges are also discussed.

Chapter 9: Conclusion and Future Scope

The final chapter summarizes the key findings of the research, highlights the contributions made, and discusses the implications of the results. It also outlines potential areas for future work and improvements in the field of handwriting-based demographic prediction.

This structure ensures a logical flow from the introduction of the research problem to the methodology, results, challenges, and conclusions providing a clear understanding of the work carried out in this thesis.

CHAPTER – 2

REVIEW OF LITERATURE

In this work, a literature review is conducted on the recognition of both Indic and Non-Indic script, with a specific focus on the application of handwritten text for predicting age, gender, and handedness through a survey protocol. The chapter begins by exploring the various challenges and techniques involved in recognizing these scripts, followed by a detailed review of publicly available datasets for both Indic and Non-Indic scripts. These datasets are crucial for developing and testing models for script recognition and classification tasks. The third section presents a compilation of studies that have investigated the classification of age, gender, and handedness using handwritten data from these scripts. Through this overview, the chapter aims to provide a comprehensive understanding of the state-of-the-art research and available resources in this field, highlighting the potential for future advancements in handwriting-based predictive modelling.

2.1 Survey Protocol

A comprehensive framework related to research work has been described on age, gender, and handedness prediction using both Indic and non- Indic scripts.

The survey follows the PRISMA (Preferred Reporting Items for Systematic Reviews and Meta-Analyses) framework to ensure a comprehensive and transparent approach to identify, select, and analyse the relevant research articles. The survey initiates with the formulation of research questions that define the scope of the review [35]. These questions mostly focus on the prediction of age, gender, and handedness through handwritten text. The survey focuses on papers published in academic journals and conference proceedings within a specified time frame. The specific journals and conferences chosen for inclusion in the survey are determined based on their reputation and prominence in the field. Figure 2.1 illustrates the PRISMA framework for selection criteria.

Various stages in the survey include its planning, sources of the dataset, the inclusion and exclusion process, as well as data extraction techniques.

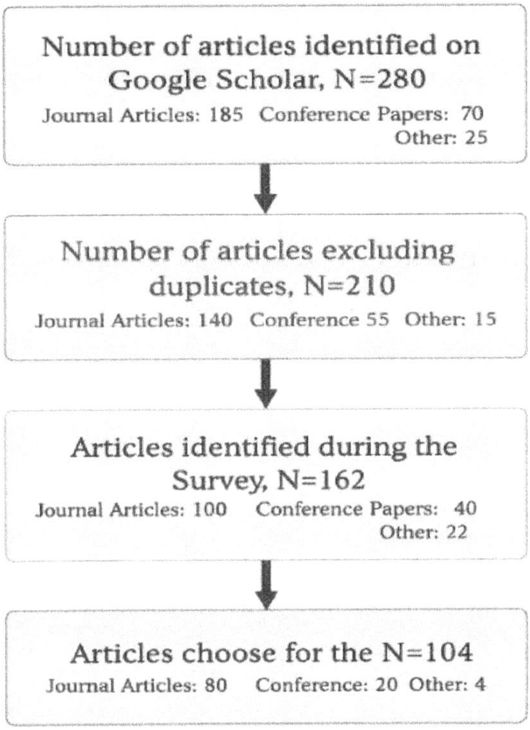

Figure 2.1: PRISMA framework for selection criteria

2.1.1 Planning the Survey

It starts with the purpose of the study, the databases used, and the techniques to recognize and validate the evidence [36]. The main goal of survey planning is to ensure smooth research so that all relevant details can be presented to achieve objectives and hidden techniques can be extracted to achieve the study's goal.

2.1.2 Inclusion and Exclusion Criteria

This phase deals with the set of rules which describe the boundaries of the research work prior to the research process being conducted. At first, inappropriate articles that were out of date were not included. Research work is only accepted if the broad field of the study is related to the topic [37-39]. High-quality journals and esteemed international conference articles were included to claim inclusion in the survey. Science Citation Indexed articles, as well as the research work of experienced researchers and professionals, are considered and more focused here. There must be a focus on both qualitative and quantitative research, and mostly the latest articles related to our work were included in the study. Irrelevant studies, which never meet our goal were individually excluded to satisfy the quality criterion.

2.1.3 Quality Assessment

After completing the inclusion and exclusion process to choose the best quality articles, a further step is to perform the quality assessment. Our topic of discussion is broad and consists of many sub-topics that require a large collection of standard SCI journals. Thus, our research work must include:

- Best quality research articles.
- Best quality dataset for both Indic and non-Indic scripts.
- Confined to the research topic.
- High-quality character recognition research.
- Feasible techniques for age, gender, and handedness prediction.
- Useful parameters for comparison of existing work.
- Suitable and efficient methods for data collection and feature extraction.

2.1.4 Data Extraction

The next step of research work is to extract useful and relevant data after analysing and interpreting the whole study. The foundation for data extraction is laid by quality assessment techniques. The major objective of data extraction is to find the essential information required for the research target to be achieved.

The data extraction method can be summed up as follows [40]:

- Firstly, the researchers reviewed all the research articles and analyse identifiers from the study that describe the primary purpose.
- After that, results were cross-checked to ensure the consistency of data extraction, and if there was any controversy, the authors held meetings to mitigate that issue.
- Data items to be studied carefully during data extraction:
- The main objective of the research.
- Bibliographic details of a journal or conference article, including author name, title, volume, and source.
- Static or dynamic mode of recognition.

- Number of writers used for the database.
- Inferences and future scope are mentioned by the researcher.

From this survey, we analysed the existing techniques for age, gender, and handedness prediction from offline handwritten test. The survey also facilitates the user regarding the importance of the system under study, how it is done and where it is helpful. This survey also provides guidance regarding the methods for data collection, data management, data analysis and outlining of the results. In this study, we determined how many scripts (Indic or non-Indic) for age, gender, and handedness classification has been successfully developed and explored various methods for feature extraction and classification helpful for the study [41]. This survey details the differences among different approaches for offline and online handwritten character recognition process. Survey analysis motivates the user for the comparative study of Indic and Non- Indic scripts and reports the reviewed work.

While numerous advancements have been made in predicting age, gender, and handedness using handwritten text analysis, it is important to acknowledge and address the limitations in this area of research. One of the primary limitations in this field is the biasness present in the datasets used for training and evaluation in terms of age range, gender, and handedness representation leads to limited generalizability of the models. Moreover, handwriting is highly subjective and can differ based on writing style, cultural background and educational level that makes it difficult to develop prediction models. Also, extracting relevant features from handwritten text has its own set of challenges. Distinct features such as slant, pressure, and curvature can be extracted that determines the most discriminative features for age, gender, and handedness prediction remains an ongoing research question. By analysing these limitations and working to mitigate them, researchers can increase the accuracy, reliability, and generalizability of prediction models in this field [42].

2.2 Recognition of both Non-Indic and Indic Scripts

The work reported under this section is based on the findings of the age, gender, and handedness predictions on both non-Indic and Indic scripts. Further, methodology adopted by researchers and limitations and challenges encountered in the existing studies has been discussed in this section. India is a diverse nation, which means it has an assortment of varied religions and cultures. The various official Indian languages are Bengali, Assamese, Hindi, Kannada, Malayalam, Marathi, Tamil, Manipuri, Maithili, Oriya, Nepali, Punjabi, Bodo, Dogri, Gujarati, Konkani, Sanskrit, Santali, Sindhi, Urdu, and Telugu. Ishida [43] analysed similar features among all scripts as they are all derived from a shared ancestor. The author mentioned certain specific aspects of Indic scripts, such as the positioning and direction of the script, independent vowels, and consonant clusters. The most used non-Indic languages, namely, Arabic, Thai, Roman, Japanese, Chinese, and Persian, have been studied for handwriting recognition.

2.2.1 Non-Indic Scripts

2.2.1.1 Arabic Script

It is an extensively used scripting language across the world. It is one of the hardest scripts in optical character recognition. The script consists of 28 letters and is written in a right-to-left manner using a cursive style. It has around 313 million native speakers across the globe. Mahmoud *et al.* [44] developed a pilot variant of the KFUPM handwritten Arabic text data-set for the research section in the field of handwritten Arabic character recognition at ICFHR 2012. This dataset was introduced by considering gender, age, and handedness prediction. There are a total of four pages in each form in the whole data set. The first page contains information about the writer, the second one consists of two paragraphs (a fixed text covering all shapes of Arabic characters and free text from 46 distinct sources), the third page contains another paragraph of randomly selected free text; and the last page consists of open data with a ruled line. El-Wakil and Shoukry [45] presented an online isolated handwritten character recognition method for the Arabic language by using a tree-like structure for pattern matching and a KNN classifier for handwriting recognition. They validated the performance of the system on 60 separated Arabic characters and achieved an accuracy of 84% for different characters and 93% for considered weights of features. Almuallim and Yamaguchi [46] mentioned a technique for identifying Arabic cursive handwriting. Here, the classification is done at the stroke level after segmenting the words into strokes. For stroke classification, topological and geometrical features have been considered, and the final word is obtained after combining the whole strokes. This method obtains a high level of accuracy on a dataset of 400 words by two writers. Bouslama and Amin [47] proposed a hybrid method for the automatic identification of Arabic characters. Different features such as curves, lines, and didactic points have been used in this work. In this article, structural methods have been employed which are being modelled by fuzzy sets. Kherallah *et al.* [48] presented an on-line Arabic handwriting recognition system that utilizes visual encoding and a genetic algorithm. The proposed system focuses on online recognition where characters are captured and processed as they are written. Using the dependent text on Arabic handwriting. Al-Maadeed *et al.* [49] created a system for writer recognition using the dependent text. The data was collected from 100 writers, and consisted of 32,000 JPEG text pictures. The extraction of features was done on the word images. Some samples of Arabic text are depicted in Figure 2.2.

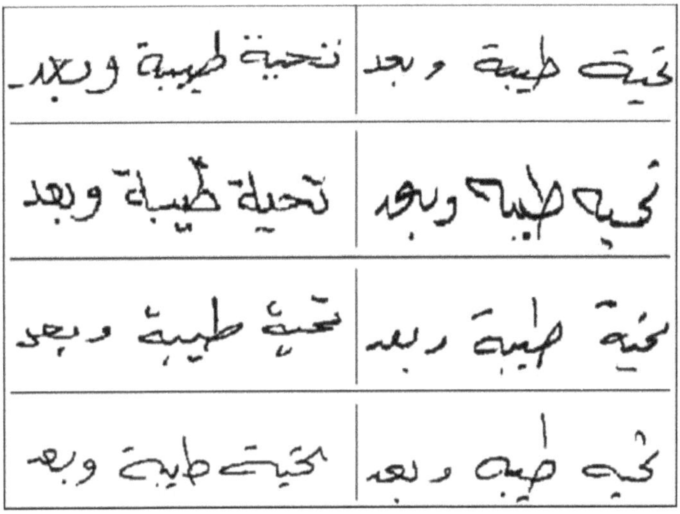

Figure 2.2: Samples of online handwritten Arabic text

2.2.1.2 Chinese Script

More than 1 billion people all around the world speak Chinese. This language is most popular among Asian people. For pattern recognition and image processing, Chinese script is quite efficient. Handwriting identification of Chinese texts seeks the interest of the researchers, as it is equally of greater interest. Chinese characters can be shown in blocks as well as in cursive writing. Bai and Huo [19] worked on the online handwritten recognition of Chinese characters. In 2005, eight directional features were used to recognize the work; these included the standardization of linear size, the addition of imaginary strokes, and the standardization of non-linear shapes, smoothing, and the equal distance of resampling. Hereby, a character sample of 64×64 was produced during this pre-processing, which is a standardized one. Following that, 8 direction features were extracted from each online character, and pattern images in 8 directions were created. After that, a feature vector with a set of 512 dimensions was produced for each character class. Finally, 99.8% is the highest accuracy they could get from this technique. He *et al.* [54] used a 2D Gabor model for offline Chinese character recognition which is an effective and normalized method. This method was quite expensive, so a new, unique method based on HMT was proposed for offline identification of Chinese character recognition. A set of information was collected by 500 people with 1,000 handwritten Chinese texts. This novel method produced an accuracy of 97.83%. Also, with this method, computation time was reduced. A few samples of Chinese script are shown in Figure 2.3.

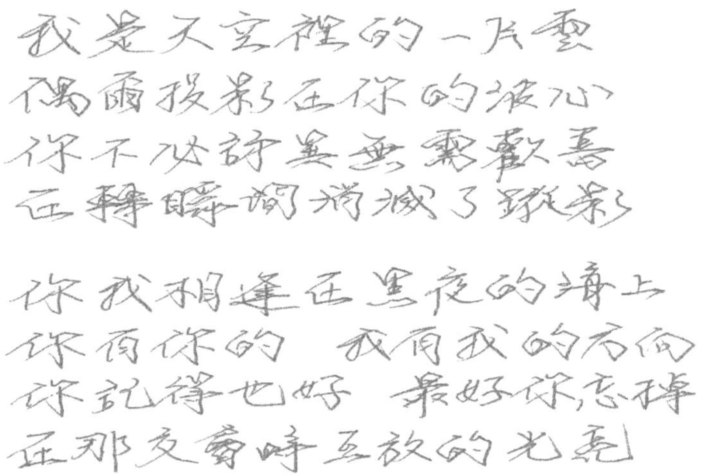

Figure 2.3: Handwritten dataset of Chinese Script

2.2.1.3 Japanese Script

This language is spoken in Japan by about 128 million people. This script makes extensive use of Chinese characters, or kanji, in its writing system. The comparison of western and Japanese online handwritten character recognition is presented by Jaeger *et al.* [50]. In their article, they elaborate on the important developments in pre-processing, classification, and post-processing stages for Japanese character recognition. Western identifiers require more complex normalization because of the changing length of western words. The nearest neighbour classifier and hidden Markov models have been used for Japanese and western handwriting, respectively. Soma *et al.* [51] have presented a study for writer identification based on handwritten offline Kanji characters. The majority voting scheme for classification as a recognizer is used for writer identification. Simulations were carried out by using an offline Kanji character database consisting of 100 Kanji characters, each written by 100 writers individually, and 50 samples of each Kanji character for a given writer. The accuracy rate obtained was 99% for a particular study. Matsumoto *et al.* [52] created an online handwritten Japanese character database with the help of 163 writers and collected 10,000-character patterns, covering 4438 categories in the context of sentences. In addition to this, the authors have evaluated this dataset in terms of stroke order, the number of strokes per character, and its changing style. Figure 2.4 illustrates some samples of handwritten Japanese characters. Soma and Arai [53] proposed a new technique for writer identification for offline handwritten Kanji characters without using features for character recognition. They have achieved an accuracy of 95.2% without rejection and 99.6% with 10% rejection for four different Kanji characters written by 100 writers.

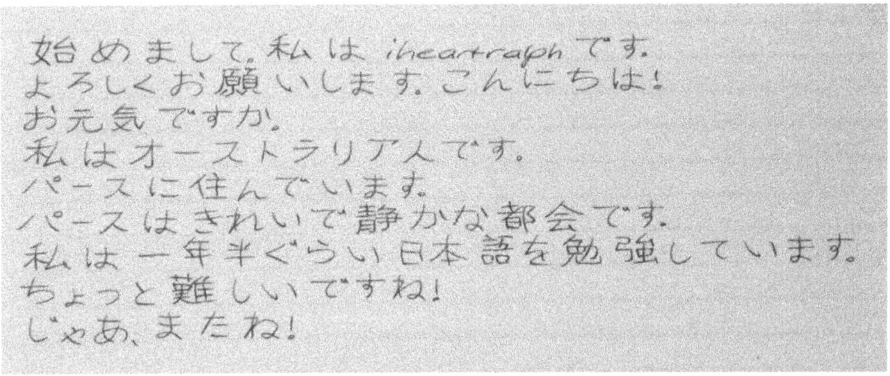

Figure 2.4: Japanese handwritten character dataset

2.2.1.4 Latin Script

Latin is an extensively used and premium language across the globe that is spoken by more than a billion people. The English language is written using the Romanian script. This script consists of 26 characters that can be used in both upper and lower case. It has a difficult writing structure, it seems like printed text, and we must write it cursively. If we write cursive, that can be jotted down in less than one go, whereas lower case takes one stroke and upper-case characters need two strokes on average. A Deep Neutral Network (Deep NN) technique was used by Chu and Srihari [35] for character recognition that recognizes the person using word level features. This is a unique method where we can identify the differences in the writing styles of different people as well as the distinct writing shapes of the same person. The ageing of character recognition was also determined. For samples of characters, 300 people writing for training and 30 scripters' writing for testing were collected. That reduced the error rate to less than 30%. For similarity of attributes in the two writings, the software CEDAR-FOX was used based on LLR (Log Likelihood Ratio). It is concluded that a greater number of samples are required for better and more accurate results. Jaeger *et al.* [4] presented NPen++ was the online handwriting recognition system. A multistate time delay neutral network (MSTDNN) approach was used to recognize the Romanian script. Several pre-processing steps were applied, like baseline computation, size normalization, missing point interpolation, and the removal of delayed strokes. All these steps were applied to raw data before extracting the features. The MSTDNN extracts feature positions in the vertical direction, pen up and down, slope, and curliness. At the state, character, and word levels, the approach was honed. Efficient tree search and pruning techniques were also reported for getting any word from big dictionaries. For a total of 5000 words in a large-size dictionary, they achieved an accuracy of 96%.

2.2.1.5 Thai Script

Another name for this language is Siamese, and it is the official language of Thailand, which is primarily used by Thai people. The words are taken from Mon, Sanskrit, Pali and old Khmer. It is spoken by around 20 million people across the world. Sanguansa *et al.* [55] presented an online Thai handwritten character recognition system using SVM and HMM classifiers. They introduced symmetric likelihood ratio score space, in which one observation series is linked to only one score. A total of 14,557 samples of characters from 42 Thai alphabets have been considered for training the classifier, written by 31 writers, and 7812-character samples for testing, written by another 62 writers. An HMM and fuzzy logic classifier for constructing an online handwritten Thai character recognition method has been introduced by Budsayaplakor *et al.* [33] after collecting 13,608 Thai character samples for training and 7664 samples for testing. Thumwarin and Matsuura [56] collected samples from 81 writers for the recognition of Thai handwritten documents. In this approach, the fourier transform approach is used as a classification method, along with the velocities of pen movements method for feature extraction. Karnchanapusaki *et al.* [57] used the linear interpolation approach for online Thai character recognition. This method helps to design a system to process and analyse Thai writing and transform it into text characters suitable for computer interpretation. The authors have implemented an arrangement of six characteristics of a Thai character, such as the head of a Thai consonant, a closed loop, the end of a Thai consonant, a twist, a straight line, and a piecewise curve. Figure 2.5 represents samples of the Thai handwriting dataset.

Figure 2.5: Thai handwritten character script

2.2.2 Indic Scripts

Indic scripts are a family of writing systems used for languages of the Indian subcontinent, primarily derived from Brahmi, one of the oldest known scripts. These scripts are characterized by a distinctive structure, often involving a horizontal line running along the top of the characters, known as a head stroke.

Figure 2.6 depicts various Indian scripts used to write Indian official languages. Most Indic scripts have been taken from Brahmi script after distinct conversions mentioned by Datta [58]. Individual scripts have been used to write varied languages, such as Bangla Script, which is used to write Assamese and Bengali. Table 2.1 displays information about India's major scripting languages, including the number of speakers and the states where they are most spoken.

Table 2.1: Major scripting languages in India with total number of speakers along with state coverage

Script	Language	Number of Speakers (In millions)	States
Tamil	Tamil	77	Tamil Nadu
Assamese	Assamese	22	Assam
Gurumukhi	Punjabi	37	Punjab
Gujarati	Gujarati	60	Gujarat
Devanagari	Hindi	692	Haryana, Rajasthan, Uttar Pradesh, Bihar, Himachal Pradesh
Oriya	Oriya	43	Orissa
Kannada	Kannada	59	Karnataka
Malayalam	Malayalam	36	Kerala
Bangla	Bengali	107	Tripura, West Bengal
Telugu	Telugu	95	Andhra Pradesh

Source: Language Atlas of India (Singh *et al.*) [59]

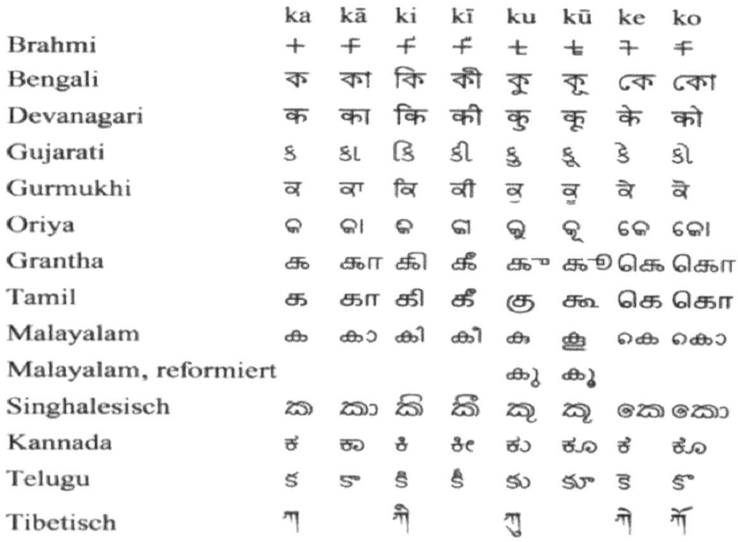

Figure 2.6: Different Indian scripts used for writing

The following subsections consist of a literature review for online and offline handwriting recognition of Indic scripts.

2.2.2.1 Assamese Script

This language is mainly used in Arunachal Pradesh and all other North-Eastern states of India. Approximately 13 million people across the globe speak this language. This language is derived from the Sanskrit script. Reddy *et al.* [76] used hidden Markov models for the recognition of online handwritten Assamese text. They collected a large amount of data from 100 writers and used 18,000 different versions of each text. The process consisted of four stages, i.e., pre-processing, feature extraction, modelling, and texting. In the pre-processing stage, size normalization, smoothing of data, interpolation of missing points, removal of duplicate points, and resampling of points were done. For feature extraction, derivatives of each point were taken as features. Each pre-processed point consisted of two coordinates, i.e., the x coordinate and the y coordinate. Their first and second derivatives were taken and further used. Half of the data was considered for the training of the classifier and the remaining half for the testing of the classifier. An accuracy of 96% was attained. Prasanna *et al.* [77] used a total of 240 Assamese characters. Out of which 11 were vowels, 40 were consonants, 147 were conjuncts, 10 were numerals, 10 were vowel modifiers, 2 were consonant modifiers, and 20 were special symbols. An online handwritten character recognizer was developed for the above characters. Strokes, sub strokes, and super strokes were used to form Assamese text. In pre-processing, on the given input data normalization of size, duplicate point removal, smoothing, interpolation of missing points, and re-sampling were done. For the feature extraction, a similar combination was used. This combination of pre-processed x and y coordinates, as well as their first and second derivatives, was used in the calculation. For the model training and recognition of labels, the hidden Markov model classifier was considered, and an online handwritten recognizer produced an efficiency of 95.2%. For the different classifiers, 81.7%, 81.6%, and 85.5% were the accuracy rates achieved for stroke, sub-stroke, and supra-stroke classifiers, respectively. The Assamese character dataset is represented in Figure 2.7.

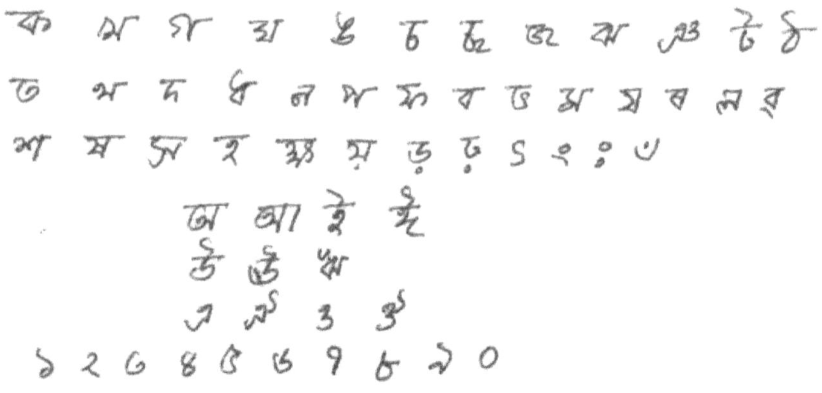

Figure 2.7: Assamese character dataset

2.2.2.2 Bangla Script

It is an Indo-Aryan language that is widely used in West Bengal and Bangladesh. It is the second most used language in India. It is one of the 22 scheduled languages of India. A lot of researchers have worked on this script. It is written horizontally from left to right. The Bengali language is a mixture of alphabetic and syllabic scripts. This language has 11 vowels, 40 consonants, and 10 numerals. Bhattacharya *et al.* [24] used a direct code-based feature extraction approach for the recognition of online Bangla handwritten characters. 114 writers wrote a net of 7043 samples of online handwritten Bangla characters. In the pre-processing activity, duplicate points were removed and all the points were re-sampled. With the use of 70 hidden nodes, the classification of characters was done with MLP (multilayer perception). The proposed recognition system achieved an accuracy of 93.9% on training data and an efficiency of 83.6% on testing data. Samanta *et al.* [75] used a hidden Markov model for the identification of online unconstrained handwritten Bangla characters. Instead of using individual sub-stroke, the whole of the word sample was taken as a basic unit for the identification. Firstly, words were separated into sub strokes. After dividing the strokes into sub strokes, features of circular, linear, and combinations of both were developed. Non-homogeneous HMMs that were fully connected were executed, and the overall efficiency is 89.7%.

2.2.2.3 Devanagari Script

This script was adapted from the Brahmi script that is mostly used in India and Nepal. Languages such as Sanskrit, Hindi, and Marathi are written in Sanskrit script in India, whereas

Nepali is written in Arabic script. Halder *et al.* ([66] proposed a technique for Devanagari script by collecting data from 50 different students. They have each written five copies of offline Devanagari characters. A 64-dimensional feature was extracted based on the gradient of the images after doing pre-processing and character extraction. For writer identification, the LIBLINEAR and LIBSVM classifiers in the WEKA environment were applied, achieving an accuracy of 99.12%. Kumar and Bhattacharya [27] used the Hidden Markov Model to identify online handwritten Devanagari script that was built based on an HMM based stroke classifier for 42 stroke classes. Swethalakshmi *et al.* [67] proposed an online handwritten character recognition system for Devanagari and Telugu script. Firstly, pre-processing was done using normalization, smoothing, and interpolation of the handwritten data. After that, a support vector machine (SVM) classifier was used to classify the stroke data that used one versus many multiclass classification strategies. This classifier used a total of 91 stroke classes. After that, a rule-based approach was utilized in the post processing phase for the recognition of Devanagari script. A total of 96.7% efficiency was achieved with the usage of 46 stroke classes and 60 features, whereas with 82 stroke classes and 120 features, an accuracy of 97.3% was achieved using this recognition system. Figure 2.8 shows the Devanagari character dataset.

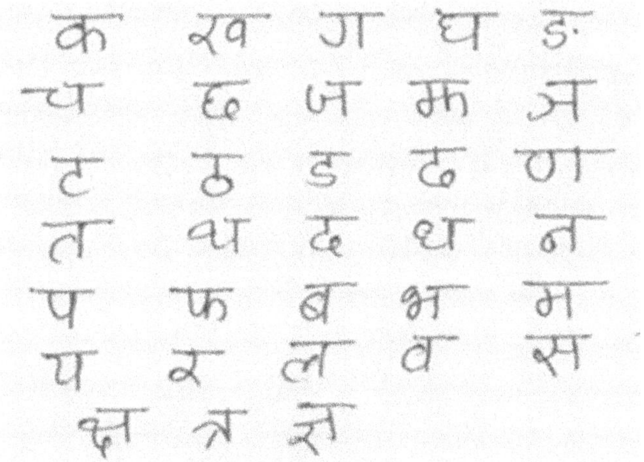

Figure 2.8: Online Devanagari handwritten character set

2.2.2.4 Gurumukhi Script

This language is used for writing the Punjabi language, and it is spoken by approximately 100 million speakers across the globe. This script has 35 basic consonants, 10 vowels, and 6 modified consonants discussed by Bahri [18]. A less comprehensive literature survey has been reported on Gurumukhi handwritten offline recognition script. Sharma *et al.* [60] started their work on online handwritten Gurumukhi script using elastic matching in two stages. Firstly, the procedure of online stroke identification has been discussed, while later, the process of forming Gurumukhi text from strokes has been mentioned. A total of 41 characters have been considered by authors, and 50 stroke levels have been formed to recognize these characters. Their proposed method using strokes was effective up to 90% for character recognition of Gurumukhi. A zone identification method was proposed by Verma and Sharma [61] for 4280 characters taken from 10 writers. For training, a stroke classifier was used using HMM to generate a five-fold validation efficiency of about 95%. Kalra and Rani [32] used the MLP classifier with 30 scripters to introduce writer recognition on Gurumukhi script and obtained an accuracy level of 53% using different feature extraction methods. Kumar *et al.* [62] showed the offline Gurumukhi handwritten characters by including open and end points, diagonals, and intersection points in their research work. HMM and Bayesian were used for classification, and testing has been done on famous printed fonts of Gurumukhi text. Sakshi *et al.* [107] used horizontal and vertical diagonal intersection points as well as power curve fitting features, as a classifier and obtained an efficiency rate of approximately 82% on 49000 samples collected from 70 scripters. Singh and Sachan [63] introduced a method of recognition of online Gurumukhi scripts using centering, size normalization, and stroke smoothing. In their article, rule-based techniques were used, and they obtained an accuracy of about 87% at Gurumukhi word level. An efficient method to produce handwritten classes on a limited set has been proposed by Singh *et al.* [64]. They used the concept of grouping, and a total of 33 names of common places in Punjab state have been considered. The authors employed the K-means clustering method and HMM and achieved an accuracy level of approximately 87% for the development of online handwritten Gurumukhi text. Kumar and Sharma [65] proposed an effective post processing algorithm for the identification of online handwritten texts of Gurumukhi. The authors used a rule-based method, and testing was done on 184 samples of the dataset. A 95.6 % accuracy rate was achieved by using the above-mentioned approach. A few samples of the Gurumukhi dataset are shown in Figure 2.9 written by 5 different writers.

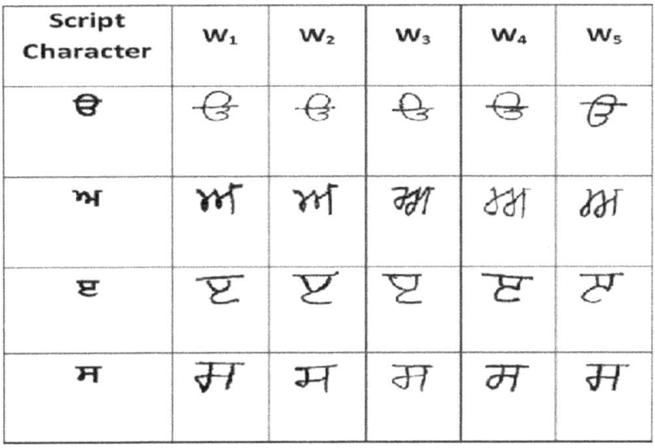

Figure 2.9: Handwritten Gurumukhi character dataset

2.2.2.5 Kannada Script

This language has its derivation from Sanskrit language. Kannada is one of the Dravidian languages that are primarily used in the south Indian state of Karnataka. Like other languages, Kannada script is written from left to right. This script consists of 16 vowels and 36 consonants. Kunwar *et al.* [78] suggested a novel technique to differentiate the recognizable characters from the online handwritten Kannada script. After the pre-processing of the input data, in the feature extraction process, extraction of some high-level features was done. At first, derivative of each point was taken; that further was classified using Statistical Dynamic Space Warping to identify Unicode characters with an accuracy rate achieved was 80%. Prasad *et al.* [79] proposed a new technique for the recognition of online handwritten Kannada script which was based on divide and conquer principle that helped in the reduction of combination of characters. First, for the separation of Kannada text into 282 different symbols, the structural and dynamic features of online handwritten Kannada text was used. Further all these symbols were segmented into three groups of different strokes, so that search space can be reduced for the recognition system. With the help of simple classifier and principal component analysis, different characteristics were taken from the stroke groups that were mapped to lower dimensional space. Combination of Kannada numerals was also considered for the first time. Genius digital notepads and tablet PCs were used to gather data and it provided efficiency of 81%. Dhandra and Vijaylaxmi [39] also mentioned a technique on Kannada text-dependent identification of writers that used structural features. Also, based on random transforms and discrete cosine transformation, a feature vector consists of multi-resolution directional spatial features. In this combination of features from two or more than that were considered and their efficiency was tested using KNN and five-fold cross validation statistics.

2.2.2.6 Malayalam Script

This language belongs to the southern part of India. It comprises a total of 73 characters, including 5 pure consonants, 4 consonant signs, 13 vowels, and 12 signs of the vowel. It is mostly related to Sanskrit and Tamil, and it is spoken by 35 million of the world's population. Shankar *et al.* [68] proposed an online handwritten identification method for Malayalam characters by extracting 18 shape features; testing has been done on a dataset of 86 strokes with 216 variations and got an efficiency of 90.8% in their proposed work. Sreeraj and Idicula [69] introduced the latest technique for character recognition in Malayalam using small written fragments of text. This technique was used on 280 writers who wrote varying numbers of pages. The authors have obtained an 89.28 % accuracy rate using the proposed method of graphemes (a small fragment of writing). Some of the work on online handwritten Malayalam text has been introduced by Namboodiri and Team [70] and they gathered 1,00,000 Malayalam words from 700 writers. For their work, the authors considered 130 classes and three feature extraction techniques such as the circular representation of strokes, histogram of gradients, and inverse curvature. For classification, SVM and LeNet- 5 CNN have been used and have achieved recognition accuracy of 96.3 % by using weighted sampling measures. Primekumar and Idiculla [71] used wavelet transformation and simplified fuzzy ARTMAP on 2530 samples of the dataset for 63 Malayalam script symbol classes in 2011. In the pre-processing phase, removal of redundant points and normalization have been incorporated, and the performance of the system has been observed using "haar" and "dbl" wavelets. They obtained the highest recognition rate of 97.8% for different Malayalam words. Different samples of the Malayalam dataset [71] are illustrated in Figure 2.9.

Figure 2.10: Malayalam handwritten dataset

2.2.2.7 Tamil Script

This language is widely spoken in Sri Lanka, Malaysia, the southern part of India, and Singapore. It is used to write in Tamil, which has 23 consonants and 12 vowels. This script is not very complex, and its writing pattern is from left to right. Thendral *et al.* [72] introduced a text dependent method of recognition for the Tamil language using different features such as local and global. They used a decision tree as a classifier and got an effectiveness of 98.6%. An online handwritten Tamil character recognition system has been proposed by Sundaram and Ramakrishnan [73] using 2-D PCA method. They used a dataset of 23,400 characters from 15 local Tamil writers. 2D-PCA is much more effective than normal PCA, as it shows a 3% improvement as compared to conventional principal component analysis. Joshi *et al.* [74] stated the comparison of matching algorithms for isolated Tamil characters using online handwriting. They have taken the dataset of 31,200 characters from 20 writers. In this proposed work, 2D coordinates have been considered and achieved satisfactory accuracy rates. Aparna *et al.* [16] presented an online handwritten Tamil character recognition system using various pre-processing states. The authors extracted a total of 18 features, including lines, dots, bumps, and so on. A dataset of 2000 samples has been used and is being written by 15 different writers. They achieved an accuracy of 82.8% for 96 classes by labelling strokes based on Tamil script. The principal component analysis method has been used by Deepu *et al.* [38] for Tamil character recognition. In this research, PCA and the nearest neighbour classifier have been used by altering distance and pre-clustering methods. The proposed work obtained an accuracy of 90.8% using a modified distance method. Figure 2.11 represents a few Tamils character dataset.

Figure 2.11: Few Tamils character dataset

2.2.2.8 Telugu script

It is a Dravidian language and is basically used in Telangana and Andhra Pradesh, along with a few neighbouring Indian states. This script is also used for writing the Sanskrit script. It consists of 35 consonants, 18 vowels, and 3 diacritics. Jayaraman *et al.* [80] identified 253 unique strokes that were used for the recognition of online handwritten Telugu text. Based on the positioning of the text, the stroke set was divided into three subclasses, i.e., baseline, bottom, and top stroker. SVM-based classifiers were used for the classification of strokers in different subclasses, and their output was compared with HMM-based classifiers. It was found that SVM classifiers performed much better in terms of efficiency as compared to HMM. For different sub-strokers, separate effectiveness was attained at 87.7% for baseline strokes, 93.1% for the bottom, and 92.80% for top strokes. Figure 2.12 represents the Telugu character dataset.

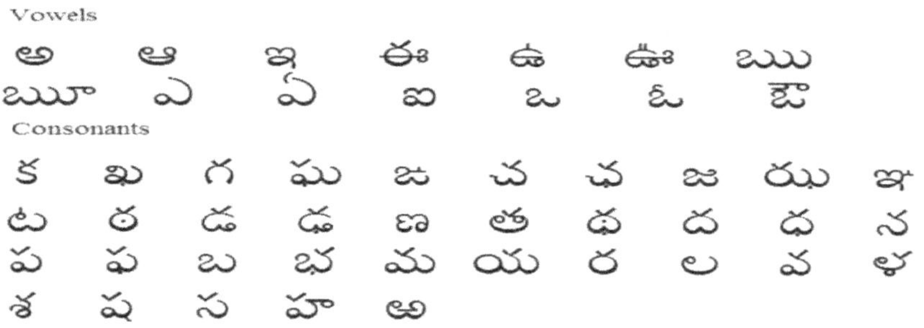

Figure 2.12 Telugu character dataset

2.3 Various Approaches

Different approaches to predict age, gender, and handedness from the handwritten text of both Indic and non-Indic scripts are mentioned below:

2.3.1 Statistical Approach

The main objective of this method is to recognize the handwriting pattern and extract information from the data based on certain statistical features. Statistical features can either be probabilistic or decision-based, which can be further categorized into two types: parametric and non-parametric methods. In a parametric approach, parameters are selected based on the training data, where each class is defined by its own set of parameters. A linear support vector machine (SVM) and hidden Markov model (HMM) classifier is a type of parametric statistical method. On the contrary, in the non-parametric approach, parameters are unknown, and it is completely distribution-free statistics. By increasing the training dataset, the complexity of non-parametric approaches increases correspondingly. The normal distribution model and KNN are examples of non-parametric methods. For easy computation and less complexity, parametric methods are mostly used in comparison with non-parametric methods. Some of the applications of this method include operational research, health sciences, machine learning, etc.

2.3.2 Structural Approach

In this approach, features are extracted from a predefined set of characters to form a feature vector having a maximum similarity level and a minimum distance. To recognize the unknown characters, a decision tree must be traversed from one node to another until the decision is finalized. This structural description is traceable to accessing the similarity among patterns. Online character recognition, knowledge sharing, social representation, and database maintenance are some of the widely known applications of the structural approach.

2.3.3 Syntactical Approach

This method deals with syntactical rules and grammar. In this pattern recognition, a formal correlation is drawn between the syntax of the language and the structure of patterns. The primitives are arranged as the alphabets of the language, and the sentences are displayed as sentences and generated as per the rules of grammar. Thus, a database of complex patterns can be recognized by the smallest number of grammatical and syntactical rules. Jain *et al.* [81] mentioned that the grammar for every pattern class must be deduced from the available training samples

2.3.4 Neural Network Approach

A neural network is a network of weighted graphs, where the edges are connections between inputs and outputs of neurons, and the nodes are artificial neurons. Its main characteristic is the potential to learn non-linear input and output relationships using linear training processes. Feed forward neural networks are mostly used for pattern classification and are composed of multi-layered Perceptron and Radial-Basis Function (RBF) networks [82]. Table 2.2 shows various pattern recognition approaches.

Table 2.2: An illustration of various approaches

Approach	Representation	Classification Method	Tools and Techniques	Criteria of Evaluation
Statistical	Using features	Discriminant analysis	SVM, KNN, HMM	Classification error
Structural	Curves, pixels, shapes	Distance measure, Correlation	Non-linear template matching	Classification error
Syntactical	Patterns and sub-patterns	Grammar, rules	Finite State Automation (FSA)	Acceptance error
Neural network	Features, pixels, graphs	Activation function	RNN, DNN, ANN	Mean Square error

2.4 List of Publicly Available Dataset for Indic and Non-Indic Scripts

Most of the datasets for Indic and non-Indic scripts are publicly available as shown in Table 2.3 along with their level of data and resources from where they have been collected.

Table 2.3: List of public datasets for Indic and Non-Indic scripts

References	Scripting Language	Dataset name	Level of data	Sources
Liu *et al.* [83]	Chinese	CASIA-OLHWDB	Characters, words	http://www.nlpr.ia.ac.cn/databases/handwriting/Download.html
Guyon *et al.* [84]	Roman	UNIPEN	Characters, words	http://unipen.org/
Mahmoud *et al.* [44]	Arabic	ONLINE-KHATT	Words	http://www.ccse.kfupm.edu.sa/dbs/onlinekhatt/index.php

Matsumoto *et al.* [52]	Japanese	Japanese character dataset	Characters	http://web.tuat.ac.jp/%7enakagawa/database/index.html
Singh *et al.* [25]	Gurumukhi	OHWR-GScript	Characters, words, Akshara's, numerals	https://sites.google.com/view/ohwr-gurmukhi-script/
Ramakrishnan and Shashidhar [85]	Kannada	MILE Lab Kannada word/symbols	Characters, words, Strokes	http://mile.ee.iisc.ac.in/
Mondal *et al.* [86]	Devanagari	Devanagari word dataset	Characters, words	https://lipitk.sourceforge.net/hpl-datasets.htm
Mondal *et al.* [86]	Tamil	Isolated Tamil word dataset	Characters, words	https://lipitk.sourceforge.net/hpl-datasets.htm,http://mile.ee.iisc.ac.in/Downloads/ohr.zip
Mondal *et al.* [86]	Bangla	ISI Bangla dataset	Characters, numerals	https://lipitk.sourceforge.net/resources.htm
Mondal *et al.* [86]	Telugu	Isolated Telugu character dataset	Characters	https://lipitk.sourceforge.net/hpl-datasets.htm

Table 2.4 summarizes key Gurumukhi handwritten character recognition studies, detailing their datasets, feature extraction approaches, classifiers, and reported accuracies. It offers a comparative view of advancements in Gurumukhi OCR research.

Table 2.4: Comprehensive overview of datasets, feature extraction methods, and recognition accuracies in Gurumukhi handwritten character recognition

References	Type (Online/ Offline)	Dataset / Samples	Features Used	Classifier / Model	Accuracy
Sharma et al. [60] (2008)	Online handwritten	41 characters	Stroke-based features	Elastic Matching (two-stage)	90.02%
Kumar & Sharma [65] (2013)	Online handwritten	184 samples	Rule-based processing features	Rule-based algorithm	95.6%
Singh & Sachan [63] (2015)	Online handwritten words	Word-level dataset	Centering, size normalization , stroke smoothing	Rule-based	~87%
Kumar et al. [62] (2016)	Offline handwritten & printed	Printed Gurumukh i fonts	End points, open points, diagonals, intersection	HMM, Bayesian	90.5%
Singh et al. [64] (2016)	Online handwritten	100 writers	Grouping + stroke analysis	K-means + HMM	~87%
Kalra & Rani [32] (2017)	Offline writer identification	30 writers	Multiple feature extraction methods	MLP	53.10%
Sakshi et al. [107] (2017)	Offline handwritten	49,000 samples, 70 writers	Diagonal intersections, power curve fitting	Naive Bayes, Decision Tree, Random Forest,	~82%

				AdaBoostM 1.	
Verma & Sharma [61] (2018)	Online handwritten	4280 characters, 10 writers	Stroke segmentation, zone identification	HMM (stroke classifier)	95.6%
Dargan & Kumar [3] (2021)	Offline handwritten	200 writers	Intersection and Open Endpoint + Curve fitting-based	SVM, MLP, KNN, Random Forest	87.76% (curve-fitting–based features)
Garg et al. [165] (2021)	Offline	8960 samples, 160 writers	Peak-extent features, Modified Division Point (MDP) features; PCA	k-NN, SVM (Linear, Polynomial, RBF)	92.3% (best with Linear-SVM, Polynomial-SVM, k-NN using 80/20 split)
Sharma et al. [166] (2024)	Offline	Gurumukhi character dataset	Novel boundary-extent feature extraction	NN, SVM	92.9%

2.5 Compiled Studies on Age, Gender and Handedness Classification based on Indic and Non-Indic Scripts

Tables 2.5, 2.6 and 2.7 depict the compiled study on Age, Gender and Handedness classification based on different Indic and Non-Indic scripts.

Table 2.5: Compiled study on age classification based on different Indic and Non-Indic scripts

Authors	Year	Script/Datasets	Features, classifiers	Accuracy
Bandi and Srihari [87]	2005	CEDAR	Neural network classifiers based on boosting and bagging	86.60%
Burger and McClusky [34]	2011	Online and offline data	Based on COHORT design	Speed / fluency of handwriting
Madeed and Hussaine [7]	2014	QUWI	Random Forest	62.40 %
Bouadjenek *et al.* [31]	2016	IAM and KHATT	SVM Classifier	78.57 % and 81.11%
Zouaoui *et al.* [88]	2017	IAM dataset	SVM Classifier	Improved accuracy
Ito *et al.* [89]	2018	Online and offline	Deep CNN	Efficient results
Basavarja *et al.* [22]	2019	IAM AND KHATT	Hu invariant moments and disconnectedness features	64.44%
Debgupta [37]	2020	IMDB-WIKI and APPA-REAL	Gradient optimization	96.27%
Pandey *et al.* [116]	2023	Gurumukhi (Punjabi)	CNN	77.20%

Table 2.6: Compiled study on gender classification based on different Indic and Non-Indic scripts

Authors	Year	Script/Datasets	Features, classifiers	Accuracy
Tomai *et al.* [90]	2004	CEDAR	KNN	70.0%

Gattal *et al.* [41]	2018	Arabic and English	Texture and discriminative features, SVM	76.0%
Liwicki *et al.* [91]	2011	Online and offline data	Gaussian Mixture Mode	65.57%
Youssef *et al.* [1]	2013	Arabic and English	Directional Features, SVM	68.6% for Arabic, 85.7% for English
PerezRosas and Mihalcea [92]	2014	Deception data from male and female	N grams, shallow, semantic and deep syntactic Classifiers	60-70 %
Bartle and Zheng [20]	2015	Blogs, Formal Handwriting	WRCNN	86%
Bouadjenek *et al.* [21]	2015	IAM Dataset	LBP, HOG	74%
Siddiqi *et al.* [93]	2015	QUWI and MSHD	ANN&SVM	68.75% - QUWI, 73.02%- MSHD
Tan *et al.* [94]	2016	ICDAR 2013 and RDF	Geometrical and transformational features	67.2%
Aubin *et al.* [17]	2018	Offline images	Graphemes, SVM	Efficient results
Najla and Suen [95]	2020	Arabic	SVM, CNN	80.05%
Rahmanian and Shayegan [8]	2021	IAM, Arabic dataset	CNN	84.0%
Maken and Gupta [96]	2021	Roman	KNN, SVM, Logarithmic Regression	Improved results

Rabaev *et al.* [97]	2021	QUWI dataset	Deep Neural Networks	76.17%
Dargan and Kumar [3]	2021	Gurumukhi (Punjabi)	SVM, MLP, KNN, Random Forest	90.57%
Qawasmeh and Suen [14]	2022	Arabic	CNN and SVM	80.05% for GoogleNet, 83.32% for ResNet
Pandey *et al.* [116]	2023	Gurumukhi	CNN	86.30%

Table 2.7: Compiled study on handedness prediction based on different Indic and Non-Indic scripts

Authors	**Year**	**Script/Datasets**	**Features, classifiers**	**Accuracy rates**
Bandi and Srihari [87]	2005	CEDAR	Neural network classifiers based on boosting and bagging	74.40%
Liwicki *et al.* [98]	2007	Online and offline	GMM	86.64%
Vander-Zant *et al.* [99]	2008	Online and offline	Textural, allographic, and placement	Improved results
Al-Maadeed *et al.* [12]	2013	QUWI database (with both English and Arabic texts)	KNN	71.5%
Saran *et al.* [100]	2013	Offline	Statistical-Analysis	Improved results

Al-Maadeed and Hassaine [7]	2014	QUWI	KNN	71.5%
Mahmoud *et al.* [101]	2014	KHATT	Hidden Markov Models (HMM)	Improved results with open database
Bouadjenek *et al.* [21]	2015	KHATT	SVM	83.93%
Griechisch and Bencsik [42]	2015	IAM Online dataset	Forensic Handwriting Experts	83.55%
Al-Maadeed *et al.* [49]	2016	QUWI	KNN	83.43%
Wang *et al.* [102]	2017	English and Chinese	CNN	80.10%
Morera *et al.* [103]	2018	IAM dataset, KHATT	CNN	90.70% and 70.91%
Akhtar *et al.* [5]	2021	Offline dataset	SVM	93.25%

2.6 Chapter Summary

This chapter presents a thorough survey on the prediction of age, gender and handedness based on handwritten text focusing on both Indic and Non-Indic scripts. It provides an in-depth exploration of the datasets available for these scripts highlighting their characteristics and the resources from which they were obtained. The chapter also includes a detailed discussion of the existing literature on age, gender and handedness prediction using handwritten samples. Furthermore, it outlines the availability and accessibility of relevant databases along with the challenges and opportunities associated with using these datasets for research and application development.

CHAPTER- 3

PHASES OF HANDWRITTEN CHARACTER RECOGNITION & EVALUATION METRICS

This chapter explores the foundational aspects of offline Handwritten Character Recognition (HCR) systems and the evaluation of models used to predict demographic features such as age, gender, and handedness. In the first section, we discuss the preliminary phases involved in developing an HCR system, covering essential processes like data collection, pre-processing, feature extraction, and the application of machine learning techniques for accurate recognition. The second section focuses on the performance evaluation metrics used to assess the predictive accuracy of models aimed at determining age, gender, and handedness from handwritten text. Together, these sections provide a comprehensive understanding of the HCR system's setup and the metrics necessary to evaluate its performance in biometric applications.

3.1 Preliminary Phases of an Offline Handwritten Character Recognition (HCR) System

The process for predicting age, gender, and handedness based on handwritten text is divided into two main stages: Training Phase and Testing Phase, followed by a Classification Phase as shown in figure 3.1. The training phase is the foundation of a handwritten character recognition system, where the model learns to recognize patterns and features from the input data. The process begins with acquiring input characters, which are pre-processed to standardize and remove noise. After pre-processing, significant features such as shape, curvature, and texture are extracted from the characters. These features are then stored in a training database, creating a comprehensive dataset for the learning process [104]. This phase is critical for developing a robust system capable of handling diverse and complex datasets.

The testing phase evaluates the performance and accuracy of the trained model on unseen data. Similar to the training phase, input characters are first pre-processed to ensure consistency with the training data. Features are extracted and saved in a testing database. The classification phase is the decision-making stage of the recognition system, where the model assigns labels to the input characters based on the extracted features.

To further enhance clarity and strengthen understanding of the proposed system, additional explanatory details have been incorporated at key stages of the workflow. A brief explanation of how normalization ensures consistency in the extracted features has been included, along with concise justification for selecting diagonal, zoning, peak-extent and transition features to clarify their relevance in character recognition. A detailed explanation of how evaluation metrics such as precision and recall behave in real-world scenarios has also been added to deepen comprehension of model performance. These enhancements improve the chapter's accessibility while maintaining its methodological and technical rigor.

3.1.1 Input Character Phase

The Input Character Phase serves as the foundation of the handwritten character recognition system. It involves two essential sub-phases: Data Collection and Digitization. These steps ensure that the system receives consistent and high-quality data for further processing.

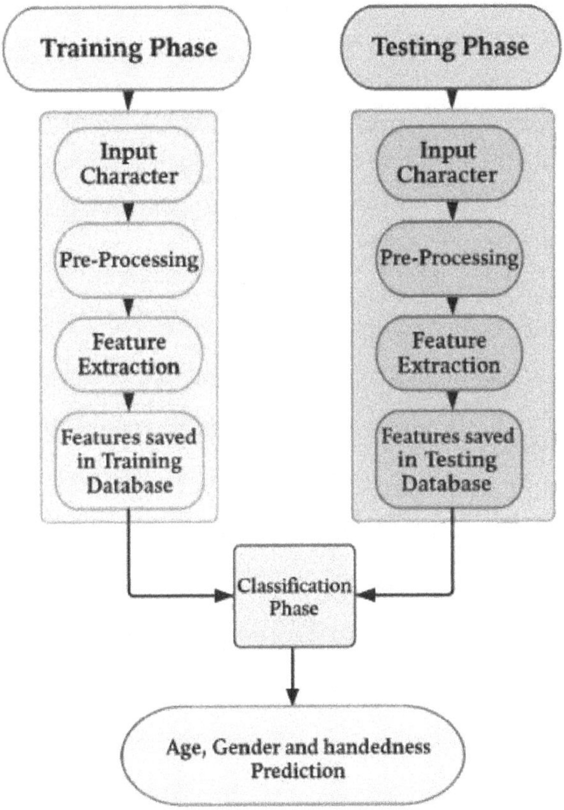

Figure 3.1 Block diagram of age, gender and handedness prediction framework

3.1.1.1 Data Collection

The study employed a comprehensive dataset comprising Gurumukhi script characters contributed by 267 individuals. Each participant, including 137 males and 130 females, provided a total of 280 Gurumukhi characters for analysis. The dataset was intentionally crafted to encompass a variety of handwriting styles, ensuring a representative sample that facilitates robust model training and evaluation. The data collection process involved procuring handwriting samples from various sources, including government offices, schools, and colleges, where each writer contributed 280 Gurumukhi characters.

3.1.1.2 Digitization

Once the handwritten data is collected, it undergoes digitization, converting it into a format suitable for computer processing. The digitization process results in a series of numerical representations and a discrete set of points for subsequent processing and analysis [105]. This transformation is facilitated through physical devices such as scanners, cameras, and other electronic tools. In our proposed system, the scanning process operates at a resolution of 300 dots per inch (dpi), a widely accepted standard value. This ensures a high-quality digitized representation of the original content, suitability for subsequent stages of analysis and application within the proposed system.

The Input Character Phase is critical for setting the stage for accurate and efficient recognition in later stages of the system. Proper execution of data collection and digitization directly impacts the quality of feature extraction and classification.

3.1.2 Pre-processing

In the pre-processing phase, the scanned documents are cleaned and normalized. The normalization process involves converting the grey-level character images into a standardized window size [106]. The resulting bitmap image is then passed through a parallel thinning algorithm, resulting in a thinned image. This process is critical for the subsequent feature extraction and classification stages of the character recognition system and serves as an essential first step in the process.

3.1.3 Feature Extraction

The feature extraction phase is a crucial step in handwriting recognition, as it helps to differentiate the age, gender, and handedness of the writer. The aim of this phase is to extract various features from the pre-segmented character image. These features provide valuable information about the character or word present in an individual's handwriting and aid in the classification process with reduced time, complexity, and computation [107].

In this phase, various features are considered for the proposed age, gender and handedness classification system including diagonal features, zoning features, peak-extent based features, and transition features. Each feature provides unique information about the handwriting allowing for more accurate gender classification.

3.1.3.1 Diagonal Features

Diagonal features are extracted by analysing patterns along the diagonal lines of the character image [108]. These features include the density of diagonal strokes or the presence of specific diagonal patterns. They help recognize slanted or diagonal strokes in characters which are crucial for languages or symbols with diagonal components.

3.1.3.2 Zoning-Based Features

The input character image is divided into several zones or regions (e.g., a grid of rows and columns). Features are extracted from each zone, capturing local characteristics such as pixel density, edges, or gradients within that region. Zoning captures spatial information about the distribution of features across different areas of the image.

3.1.3.3 Peak-Extent Features

Peak-extent features refer to a method of extracting character features by analysing the extremities of the character in terms of peaks, valleys, or extents in the vertical and horizontal directions. These features help in understanding the structural outline of the character [109].

3.1.3.4 Transition Features

Transition features analyse changes in pixel intensity or other attributes as you move across a row or column in the image. For example, the number of times a black-to-white or white-to-black transition occurs. They capture boundary information and help detect edges or shapes within the character image.

3.1.3.5 Hybridization of Feature Extraction Techniques

The hybridization of multiple feature extraction techniques is a powerful approach to improve the accuracy and robustness of character recognition systems. Combining different methods allows the system to capture diverse aspects of the character's structure and spatial distribution, which may not be fully represented by a single technique.

In particular, the integration of diagonal features, zoning features, peak-extent features, and transition features provides a comprehensive feature set for character recognition. This integration ensures that both global and local characteristics are captured, enhancing the system's ability to recognize diverse and complex characters. Hybridization also improves classification accuracy by leveraging multiple aspects of the character's geometry and spatial distribution, reducing the likelihood of misclassification. Additionally, it increases robustness to variations in handwriting styles, fonts, and noisy data, as different features compensate for each other's weaknesses. For example, while zoning features focus on localized details, peak-extent features preserve the overall structure, and transition features capture edge boundaries. This complementary nature makes hybrid systems well-suited for challenging tasks, such as recognizing handwritten text or characters from multiple scripts.

3.1.4 Classification

The classification phase in handwriting analysis involves the process of categorizing handwritten text into predefined classes based on certain features and patterns identified during feature extraction [110-112]. This phase is a crucial step in many applications such as age, gender, and handedness prediction, where the goal is to assign the handwritten sample to an appropriate category or group based on learned characteristics.

In the classification phase, once the relevant features (such as stroke direction, pressure, consistency, slant, and spacing) have been extracted from the handwriting, machine learning algorithms are applied to classify the input data. Common classifiers used in this phase include support vector machines (SVM) [113], Multilayer Perceptron's (MLPs), K-nearest neighbours (KNN), Random Forests, and Convolutional Neural Networks (CNN) [114]. These classifiers analyse the extracted features and use a trained model to make predictions or assign the input data to one of the classes.

For example, in age classification, the model may categorize handwriting into different age groups based on features like letter size and pressure. In gender classification, the classifier might differentiate between male and female handwriting based on characteristics such as slant and curvature of strokes. In handedness prediction, the classifier identifies whether the individual is left- or right-handed by examining the direction of strokes and the overall writing style. The classification phase can be implemented through supervised learning, where the model is trained on labelled data, or through unsupervised learning, where the model tries to find inherent patterns in unlabelled data.

The accuracy of the classification phase depends on the quality of the feature extraction process, the choice of the classifier, and the dataset used for training. This phase often involves evaluation metrics such as accuracy, precision, recall, and F1-Score to assess the performance of the classification model [115].

3.1.4.1 Support Vector Machine (SVM)

Support Vector Machine (SVM) is a supervised machine learning algorithm widely used for classification and regression tasks, especially when dealing with high-dimensional data [113]. SVM works by finding a hyperplane that best separates the data into different classes, aiming to maximize the margin between the classes. This separation is achieved by focusing on the support vectors—data points that lie closest to the hyperplane. In cases where data is not linearly separable, SVM uses the kernel trick to map data into a higher-dimensional space, allowing for linear separation in this transformed space. Popular kernel functions include the polynomial, radial basis function (RBF), and sigmoid kernels. SVM is particularly known for its ability to handle non-linear data, and it performs well with high-dimensional datasets, making it suitable for applications like text and handwriting recognition. However, it can be computationally expensive, especially for large datasets, and selecting the right kernel and tuning parameters such as C (which controls the trade-off between maximizing the margin and minimizing misclassification) can be challenging. Despite these drawbacks, SVM is highly regarded for its ability to create robust classifiers, particularly when the data is clearly separable and when the risk of overfitting is low.

3.1.4.2 Multilayer Perceptron's (MLPs)

A Multilayer Perceptron (MLP) is a type of artificial neural network that consists of multiple layers of nodes, or "neurons," each of which is connected to the nodes in the previous and subsequent layers. MLPs are a subset of feedforward neural networks, meaning that the information moves in one direction—from the input layer to the output layer—without cycles. Typically, an MLP consists of three types of layers: the input layer, the hidden layers, and the output layer [114].

Each neuron in the MLP performs a mathematical operation, usually involving weighted sums of the inputs followed by a non-linear activation function, such as the sigmoid, ReLU (Rectified Linear Unit), or tanh functions. The hidden layers allow the network to model complex, non-linear relationships between the input and output. The number of hidden layers and neurons in each layer can vary depending on the complexity of the task at hand.

3.1.4.3 K-Nearest Neighbours (KNN)

K-Nearest Neighbours (KNN) is a simple, yet powerful, supervised machine learning algorithm used for classification and regression tasks. The core idea behind K-NN is that it classifies a data point based on the majority class (for classification) or the average value (for regression) of its k nearest neighbours in the feature space. These neighbours are determined based on a distance metric, typically Euclidean distance, but other metrics such as Manhattan or Minkowski distance can also be used depending on the problem [116].

During the prediction phase, when a new data point needs to be classified or predicted, the K-NN algorithm calculates the distance between the point and all other points in the training dataset. It then selects the k closest data points (neighbours) and uses their labels or values to make a prediction. For classification tasks, the label that appears most frequently among the k neighbours is assigned to the data point. In regression tasks, the prediction is usually the average of the values of the k nearest neighbours.

One of the key advantages of K-NN is its simplicity, as it does not require any model training. It is an instance-based learning algorithm, meaning that it makes predictions based on the stored training data.

3.1.4.4 Random Forest

Random forest is an ensemble learning algorithm primarily used for classification and regression tasks. It works by creating a multitude of decision trees during training and then combining their outputs to make more accurate predictions. The strength of Random Forest lies in its ability to reduce overfitting, which is a common issue in individual decision trees, while maintaining high accuracy and robustness.

In the training phase, Random Forest constructs several decision trees, where each tree is built using a random subset of the training data (bootstrapping) and a random subset of features at each decision node [117-119]. This randomness helps ensure that the trees are diverse and reduces the risk of overfitting to any subset of the data. Once the trees are trained, for classification tasks, each tree casts a vote for the predicted class, and the class that receives the majority of votes is chosen as the final prediction. For regression tasks, the average of all the tree predictions is used.

One of the key advantages of Random Forest is that it can handle large datasets with high dimensionality and still deliver accurate predictions. Additionally, it provides useful measures like feature importance which helps identify the most influential features in the data.

3.1.4.5 Convolutional Neural Networks (CNNs)

Convolutional Neural Networks (CNNs) are a class of deep learning algorithms designed specifically for processing structured grid data, such as images, audio, and video. CNNs are highly effective in image recognition, object detection, and computer vision tasks due to their ability to automatically learn spatial hierarchies of features from raw data [120]. The architecture of a CNN typically includes convolutional layers, which apply filters to detect patterns like edges or textures in the input image; activation layers, usually using ReLU (Rectified Linear Unit), which introduce non-linearity to help learn complex patterns; and pooling layers that reduce the spatial dimensions of the feature maps, making the model more computationally efficient as illustrated in figure 3.2. At the end of the network, fully connected layers and an output layer are used for classification or prediction tasks. CNNs are powerful in capturing spatial dependencies and features, which makes them ideal for visual data analysis.

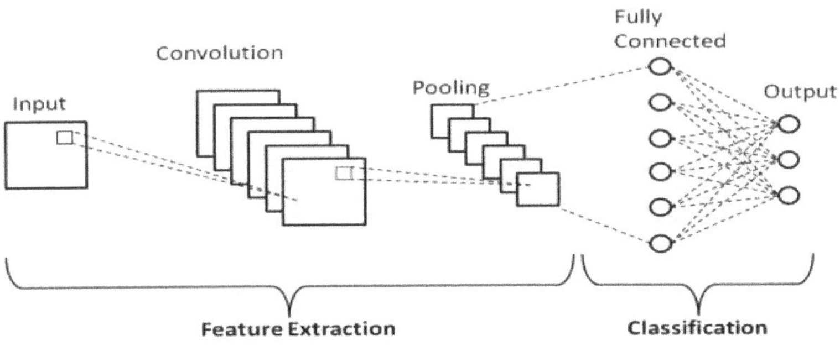

Figure 3.2: Convolutional neural network architecture

3.2 Performance Evaluation Metrics in Age, Gender and Handedness Prediction

In the domain of handwritten character recognition, particularly for applications like age, gender, and handedness prediction, performance evaluation metrics are essential tools for assessing the accuracy and reliability of predictive models [121-122]. These metrics help determine how well a model generalizes to new, unseen data ensuring its practical applicability in real-world scenarios. For age, gender, and handedness prediction, performance metrics provide insights into how well the model identifies patterns in handwriting related to demographic features, which can be a challenging task due to the variability in handwriting styles, font types, and noise in the data.

The following are key performance evaluation metrics commonly used to assess the effectiveness of age, gender, and handedness prediction systems:

3.2.1 Accuracy

Accuracy is the most straightforward metric, representing the percentage of correct predictions made by the model out of all predictions [123]. It is calculated as:

$$Accuracy = \frac{Total\ Number\ of\ Predictions}{Number\ of\ correct\ Predictions}$$

In age, gender, and handedness prediction systems, accuracy indicates how often the model successfully classifies a given sample into the correct category (age group, gender, or handedness). While accuracy is a valuable metric, it can be misleading in cases of imbalanced datasets where certain categories may dominate, so it should be interpreted alongside other metrics.

3.2.2 Precision

Precision measures the proportion of correct positive predictions (true positives) relative to the total number of positive predictions made by the model (true positives + false positives) [124]. It is particularly important when false positives are costly or undesirable.

$$Precision = \frac{True\ Positives}{True\ positives + false\ positivites}$$

Here,

True Positives (TP): The number of correct predictions for the target class.

True Negatives (TN): The number of correct predictions for the non-target class.

False Positives (FP): The number of incorrect predictions where the model incorrectly labels a sample as the target class.

False Negatives (FN): The number of incorrect predictions where the model fails to identify a sample as the target class.

In the context of age, gender, and handedness prediction, precision is useful in evaluating how accurately the system classifies each category. For example, in predicting gender, a higher precision Score means fewer incorrect gender predictions, which is important when the cost of a misclassification is high.

3.2.3 Recall (Sensitivity)

Recall, also known as sensitivity or true positive rate, measures the proportion of actual positives that are correctly identified by the model.

$$Recall = \frac{True\ Positives}{True\ positives + false\ negatives}$$

For age, gender, and handedness prediction, recall is essential when it is more important to correctly identify as many positive instances (correct class labels) as possible, even if some of them are misclassified. For example, in age prediction, a high recall value ensures that most individuals in the targeted age group are accurately classified, which is crucial for certain demographic-based applications [125-127].

3.2.4. F1-Score

The F1-Score is the harmonic mean of precision and recall, providing a balance between the two metrics. It is especially useful when dealing with imbalanced datasets where one class is more prevalent than others. The F1-Score combines both precision and recall into a single metric, making it easier to assess overall performance.

$$F1 - Score = \frac{2 \times Precision \times Recall}{Precision + Recall}$$

For a balanced trade-off between false positives and false negatives, F1-Score is often considered a more informative measure than accuracy [128]. It is critical in cases where the costs of false positives and false negatives are both significant, such as in gender or age classification based on handwriting.

3.2 Chapter Summary

This chapter provides an overview of two crucial aspects: the preliminary phases of an offline Handwritten Character Recognition (HCR) system and the performance evaluation metrics for predicting age, gender, and handedness. It begins by outlining the essential steps in developing an HCR system, including data collection, pre-processing, feature extraction, and model selection. These steps form the foundation for accurate character recognition. The chapter then shifts focus to the evaluation of predictive models, discussing key performance metrics such as accuracy, precision, recall, and F1-Score. These metrics are critical in assessing the effectiveness of age, gender, and handedness predictions, while also addressing the challenges in evaluating handwritten data variability.

CHAPTER- 4

PROPOSED METHODOLOGY FOR AGE, GENDER & HANDEDNESS PREDICTION USING CNN

This chapter focuses on the methodology used to develop a technique for predicting age, gender, and handedness from offline handwritten Gurumukhi text. Age prediction focuses on analysing stroke dynamics, writing pressure and geometric traits that reflect age-related motor and cognitive characteristics. Gender prediction examines stylometric features such as curvature, stroke thickness, and spatial alignment, which often differ based on physiological and stylistic variations. Handedness prediction relies on spatial orientation, slant patterns, and character positioning, which are indicative of left- or right-hand dominance. The chapter details the processes of data pre-processing, feature extraction and the application of machine learning models by providing a systematic approach to demographic analysis through handwriting.

4.1 Age Classification (Proposed Method-I)

Age classification using handwriting analysis has made significant interest across various domains, including forensics, education, and biometrics. The ability to estimate or classify the age group of an individual based on handwriting can provide critical insights into personal identification, cognitive assessment, and other psychological studies. This chapter explores the methodology, dataset, model architecture, implementation, results, and implications of using Convolutional Neural Networks (CNNs) for age classification based on handwriting samples in Gurumukhi script.

4.1.1 Overview of Handwriting-Based Age Classification

Handwriting is a complex motor skill influenced by a combination of neuromuscular, cognitive, and perceptual factors [129-132]. These factors evolve with age, making handwriting a potentially reliable biomarker for age classification. Variations in handwriting features such as letter formation, size, spacing, and pressure provide clues to the writer's developmental stage. Previous studies have demonstrated the feasibility of age classification using traditional machine learning methods, but advancements in deep learning offer more robust and accurate solutions.

This research uses pre-segmented offline Gurumukhi characters as input features to train a CNN model for classifying writers into predefined age groups. Gurumukhi script, primarily used for Punjabi language writing, is a syllabic script characterized by unique curves, loops and strokes that vary among individuals and across age groups.

4.1.2 Dataset Description

The study utilized a dataset comprising 74,760 Gurumukhi characters collected from 267 writers, including 137 males and 130 females. The dataset was categorized into three age groups:

- 5-10 years: Young children developing handwriting skills.
- 11-15 years: Adolescents with improved motor control and handwriting stability.
- 16-20 years: Young adults exhibiting more refined handwriting.

Each participant contributed 280 characters, ensuring a balanced representation across all categories. The handwriting samples were carefully pre-processed to extract individual characters while preserving their structural integrity. This segmentation process was crucial for achieving high-quality input data for the CNN model.

4.1.3 Model Architecture and Implementation

The age classification model used the Inception-V3 architecture, a state-of-the-art CNN model known for its ability to extract hierarchical and abstract features from input data. Inception-V3 is particularly well-suited for image analysis tasks due to its modular structure and multi-scale feature extraction capabilities.

In this process, Inception-V3 serves as a feature extractor, tasked with extracting high-level and discriminative features from pre-segmented offline handwritten Gurumukhi characters [121]. These characters are utilized as input to the network, and the intermediate layers of Inception V3 capture the hierarchical representations of these characters. Subsequently, the extracted features are channeled into a classification layer, comprised of fully connected layers, to predict the age group of the writer. By using Inception V3 both as a feature extractor and a classifier, the proposed approach benefits from the model's capacity to learn and represent intricate patterns within the Gurumukhi characters. This, in turn, enables precise age classification based on the features extracted from the pre-segmented characters. The integration of Inception V3 as both a feature extractor and classifier within the CNN architecture elevates the performance of the age classification system, furnishing accurate predictions founded on the characteristics of the Gurumukhi handwriting samples.

Learning Rate: The learning rate plays a pivotal role in determining the step size at which the model's parameters are updated during training. A higher learning rate may expedite convergence but heightens the risk of overshooting the optimal solution, while a lower learning rate may lead to slower convergence. Finding the appropriate learning rate often involves experimentation to strike the right balance [133].

Batch Size: The batch size dictates the number of samples processed in each iteration during training. A larger batch size can result in more stable parameter updates but demands more memory. Conversely, a smaller batch size can introduce more noise during training but requires less memory [134-136]. It is crucial to find an appropriate batch size that strikes a balance between computational efficiency and model performance.

Number of Epochs: The number of epochs represents how many times the entire training dataset is traversed by the network during training [137]. Increasing the number of epochs allows the model to learn more from the data, but there is a risk of overfitting if the model begins to memorize the training samples excessively. The ideal number of epochs is typically determined through a combination of experimentation and validation performance assessment

Dropout rate: Adjusting the regularization coefficient or dropout rate enables control over the strength of regularization, based on the dataset's complexity and the risk of overfitting [138-140].

Activation function: The choice of activation functions in the network's layers can impact its learning capacity. In Inception-V3, commonly used activation functions such as ReLU (Rectified Linear Unit) are used [141]. However, exploring different activation functions, including variants of ReLU or other nonlinear functions, may lead to improved performance for specific tasks or datasets.

The general structure of the proposed methodology is depicted in Figure 4.1. A brief overview of each operation conducted within the proposed methodology is provided below.

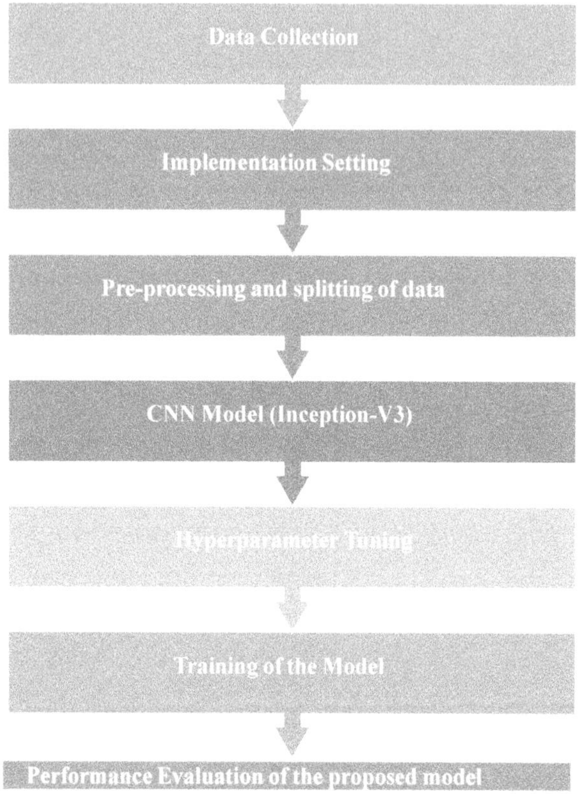

Figure 4.1: Proposed method

The model was implemented in the Google Collaboratory environment using Python and the Keras deep learning library. Key steps in the implementation process included:

I. Data Pre-processing

- Normalizing the grayscale images of Gurumukhi characters.
- Resizing the images to match the input dimensions required by the Inception-V3 model.
- Splitting the dataset into 70% training data and 30% testing data.

The training set is allocated 70% of the data with the remaining 30% assigned to the testing set, as depicted in Table 4.1.

Table 4.1: Number of training and testing sample images

Dataset Used	Number of Samples	Training Samples	Testing Samples
Offline Gurumukhi	74760	52332	22428

II. Model Training

- Using categorical cross-entropy as the loss function to handle multi-class classification.
- Using the Adam optimizer to achieve efficient convergence.
- Setting a batch size of 32 and training the model over 50 epochs.

Table 4.2 outlines the model hyperparameters that should be considered when using Inception-V3 for age classification based on handwriting samples.

Table 4.2: Model Hyper parameters chosen for the proposed approach

Learning Rate	Batch Size	Number of Epochs	Dropout rate	Activation Function
0.001	32	30	0.25	ReLU

III. Feature Extraction

- Utilizing the convolutional layers of Inception-V3 to extract meaningful patterns, including edges, textures, and structural nuances unique to each age group.

IV. Classification Layer

- Adding fully connected layers with a SoftMax activation function to classify the input into one of the three age groups [142-143].

4.1.4 Experimental Results

The trained model achieved an accuracy rate of 92.7% on the test set demonstrating its ability to classify handwriting samples into age groups effectively. This high accuracy underscores the effectiveness of combining deep learning techniques with pre-segmented handwriting data for age classification.

Key observations from the results include:

- **High Accuracy for Older Age Groups:** The model performed exceptionally well in classifying samples from the 16-20 years age group, likely due to the more consistent and refined handwriting characteristics in this category [144-145].
- **Moderate Challenges with Younger Age Groups:** While the accuracy for the 5-10 years age group was slightly lower, the model still demonstrated a strong ability to distinguish between immature and intermediate handwriting traits [146].
- **Balanced Dataset Contribution:** The balanced representation of characters across all age groups contributed to the robustness of the model.

4.1.5 Implications and Applications

The findings of this study have significant implications for various fields:

- **Forensics:** Age classification can assist in identifying individuals based on anonymous handwritten notes supporting criminal investigations and forensic analysis.
- **Education:** Schools and educators can use handwriting-based age classification to assess students' motor skill development and cognitive growth.
- **Biometrics:** Handwriting analysis can enhance existing biometric systems by providing an additional layer of security and verification.
- **Healthcare:** Age estimation through handwriting can support early detection of developmental delays or neurological disorders.

4.2 Gender Classification (Proposed Method-II)

The gender classification task like age classification, is approached using Convolutional Neural Networks (CNNs). However, this section focuses specifically on the adaptation of the CNN model for distinguishing gender from handwritten Gurumukhi characters. We will outline the model's specific architecture adjustments, training procedure, and evaluation metrics for this task.

4.2.1 Adjustments for Gender Classification

While the architecture of the CNN remains similar to the one used for age classification, the gender classification task requires tailoring the network to identify gender-specific patterns in the handwriting. In this case, rather than predicting multiple age categories, the model must predict one of two possible classes: male or female. As a result, the final output layer is adjusted to have two nodes corresponding to these classes.

Additionally, given the relatively binary nature of the problem, we focus on refining the data pre-processing steps to ensure that subtle features relevant to gender differences in handwriting are accurately captured. These include focusing on certain characteristics that might differentiate male and female handwriting styles, such as stroke angles, character slant, and overall shape variations.

4.2.2 Gender-Specific Feature Extraction

Gender classification in handwriting typically involves subtle differences in writing style. Therefore, the convolutional layers in the CNN are key to extracting gender-specific features from the handwritten characters [147]. These features may include:

- Character Slant: Gender-specific handwriting often exhibits differences in the slant or angle of the characters.
- Stroke Thickness: Male handwriting may exhibit thicker strokes due to greater pressure, while female handwriting may have thinner, more precise strokes.
- Spacing: Handwriting characteristics such as the amount of space between characters can vary between genders.

These differences, though subtle may provide the discriminative power needed for gender classification. The CNN, through its hierarchical structure, learns to detect these patterns automatically from the raw image data.

4.2.3 Model Training

For the gender classification model, we use the same dataset of 74,760 Gurumukhi characters, segmented into images of individual handwritten characters. The dataset is split into training and validation sets with an 80/20 ratio. The model is trained in a supervised manner using labelled data for both male and female characters. The binary cross-entropy loss function is employed due to the binary nature of the classification task.

The optimizer of choice is the Adam optimizer which adapts the learning rate for each parameter during training, helping the model converge more efficiently. The model is trained over a series of epochs, with early stopping applied to prevent overfitting.

Data augmentation is used to create variability in the training set, ensuring the model does not memorize specific features but instead generalizes well to unseen examples. This includes random rotations, translations, and scaling which help the model become more robust to variations in handwriting [148-150].

4.2.3.1 Methodology Adopted

Figure 4.2 shows the step-wise framework for gender classification system.

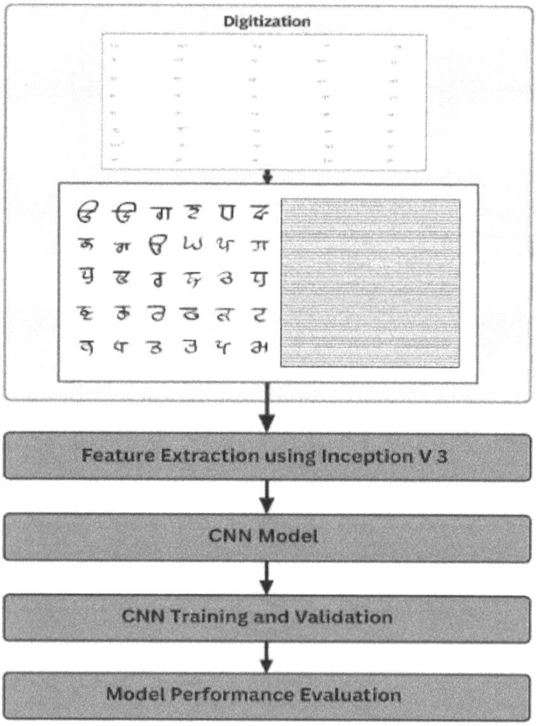

Figure 4.2: Framework for gender classification system

i. Digitization

The digitization process results in a series of numerical representations and a discrete set of points for subsequent processing and analysis [151]. This transformation is facilitated through physical devices such as scanners, cameras, and other electronic tools. In our proposed system, the scanning process operates at a resolution of 300 dots per inch (dpi), a widely accepted standard value. This ensures a high-quality digitized representation of the original content, suitability for subsequent stages of analysis and application within the proposed system.

ii. Pre-processing

Prior to training the Convolutional Neural Network [114], a pre-processing pipeline is executed to enhance the data quality. This entails normalizing handwriting samples to a standardized size, eliminating noise, and employing a pre-segmentation process to extract individual Gurumukhi characters. The goal is to ensure uniformity and precision in character extraction, promoting effective feature representation during the subsequent stages of analysis.

Slicing Phase

In this phase, the initial step entails adjusting the threshold value to convert the black and white values of the scanned Gurumukhi characters into a binary image. Following this, the slicing process is applied to the converted image. The Gurumukhi characters, handwritten by various contributors on a sheet, undergo scanning and are subsequently segmented into individual characters. Each character is then stored separately in a dedicated folder, identified uniquely for subsequent processing, as illustrated in Figure 4.3.

Figure 4.3: Sliced data

The objective of this phase is to streamline the analysis of individual characters. Given that the processing is conducted independently for each character, this phase transforms a single-page document into an array of distinct characters. The process includes the removal of blank spaces, ensuring the isolation of each character, which is then stored in a structured format. This prepares the data for more comprehensive analysis and feature extraction in subsequent stages of the methodology.

Normalization Phase

Normalization is a pivotal step in the data preparation process, entailing the adjustment of numeric column values within a dataset to a standardized scale without compromising essential information [152]. As a form of scaling, this process rescales and shifts values to a common range, usually between 0 and 1. In this phase of the study, Gurumukhi characters undergo normalization within a window of dimensions 64×64. The primary objective is to ensure uniformity among characters, fostering similar distributions across the dataset.

After normalization, the next step involves converting .gif images to. bitmap images. This conversion is facilitated through online tools, preserving essential characteristics while transforming the image format. The conversion process enhances the standardization and compatibility of the dataset, aligning with the requirements of the subsequent stages of analysis and feature extraction in the research methodology [153].

iii. Feature Extraction

Extracting discriminative features from Gurumukhi characters stands as a crucial step in the methodology. Features including slant, curvature, and spatial relationships are computed to capture the distinctive characteristics associated with each script [154]. The Inception-V3 model, renowned for its effectiveness in image recognition, is used to automatically learn hierarchical representations of these features from the pre-processed Gurumukhi characters.

iv. Convolutional Neural Network (CNN) Architecture

The gender classification system was implemented utilizing a CNN architecture with the Inception-V3 model. The network included convolutional layers for feature extraction, pooling layers for dimensionality reduction, and fully connected layers for gender classification [27]. The selection of the Inception-V3 model enabled the system to capture intricate patterns in Gurumukhi characters, thereby enhancing its capability to discern gender-specific writing styles.

v. Training and Validation

The dataset underwent division into training and validation sets to enable effective model training and evaluation. Employing backpropagation, the CNN model was trained to optimize weights based on a specified loss function. Throughout training, the model iteratively adjusted its parameters to minimize the disparity between predicted and actual gender labels [28]. The validation set played a crucial role in assessing the model's generalization performance and mitigating the risk of overfitting.

vi. Evaluation Metrics

After training, the model's performance is evaluated using the validation set. The primary evaluation metric is accuracy, but additional metrics like precision, recall, and F1-Score are also computed to provide a more comprehensive analysis of the model's ability to correctly classify gender.

- Precision: Measures how many of the predicted male (or female) characters were correct.
- Recall: Measures how many of the actual male (or female) characters were correctly predicted.
- F1-Score: Provides a balanced measure of precision and recall, useful when the dataset is imbalanced.

The performance of the model is visualized using a confusion matrix which highlights the true positives, false positives, true negatives, and false negatives, allowing for a more detailed analysis of the model's errors.

4.2.4 Results and Discussion

The gender classification CNN model achieved an accuracy of 94.22%. This indicates that the model was able to correctly classify the gender of handwritten Gurumukhi characters with high precision.

In terms of precision and recall, the model achieved values of 94.1% and 94.3%, respectively, which suggests that it is both accurate and balanced in its predictions. The F1-Score of 94.2% further confirms that the model performs well across both gender categories.

The confusion matrix revealed that most misclassifications occurred between the two classes, but the overall number of errors was low, highlighting the model's reliability [155].

4.3 Handedness Prediction (Proposed Method-III)

The task of predicting handedness from handwritten characters presents a significant challenge, especially when applied to the Gurumukhi script. The key problem addressed by this study is the development of an effective model capable of predicting whether a person is left-handed or right-handed based on their handwriting in this complex script. The variation in individual handwriting styles combined with the intricacy of the script itself, makes it difficult to directly correlate handwriting features with handedness [156-158].

The overview of the proposed method for handedness prediction is illustrated in Figure 4.4.

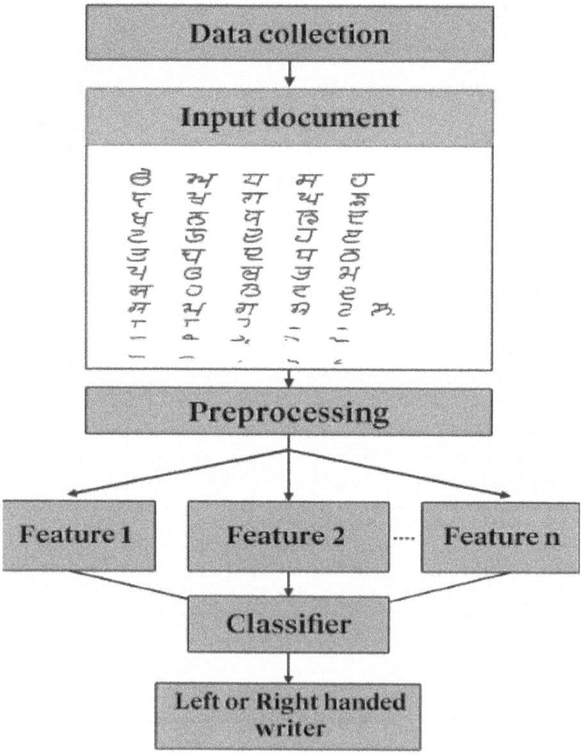

Figure 4.4 Overview of the proposed handedness approach

4.3.1 Experimental Results

Upon training the predictive model using a supervised learning approach, several performance metrics were evaluated, including accuracy, precision, recall, and F1-Score. The model achieved an impressive accuracy of 91.70%, indicating its capability to accurately predict handedness based on Gurumukhi characters. In addition to accuracy, the model also attained a precision of 90.3%, recall of 88.65%, and an F1-Score of 91.2%. These metrics highlight the model's balanced performance in terms of both precision (the proportion of true positive predictions among all positive predictions) and recall (the proportion of true positive predictions among all actual positives).

To further validate the effectiveness of the proposed methodology, a k-fold cross-validation approach was employed, ensuring that the model's performance was consistent across different subsets of the data. The results from the cross-validation corroborated the initial findings demonstrating the model's stability and reliability in various folds of the dataset.

Additionally, a study was conducted to assess the contribution of hybrid features to the overall performance of the model. By selectively removing certain feature types and re-evaluating the model, it was observed that the inclusion of both basic stroke patterns and complex structural elements significantly enhanced the predictive accuracy. This confirms the importance of using a hybrid CNN architecture for extracting comprehensive features from handwritten Gurumukhi characters.

The proposed approach also exhibits scalability, as it can be applied to larger datasets and extended to other handwriting analysis tasks. By using the power of CNNs to capture intricate handwriting features, the methodology holds promise for broader applications in the field of handwriting recognition and analysis.

4.3.1.1 Discussion

The results confirm that the hybrid CNN model is highly effective for predicting handedness from handwritten Gurumukhi characters. The model's superior performance can be attributed to the use of deep learning techniques that automatically extract relevant features, which traditional methods struggle to capture. The model also demonstrated robustness across various writers, suggesting its potential for real-world applications.

4.4 Summary of the Chapter

This chapter presented a methodology for predicting age, gender, and handedness from offline handwritten Gurumukhi text. It focused on using stroke dynamics, writing pressure, and geometric features for age prediction, stylometric characteristics for gender prediction, and spatial orientation for handedness classification. The chapter detailed the steps involved in data pre-processing, feature extraction, and model training using Convolutional Neural Networks (CNNs). For age classification, the Inception-V3 architecture was employed to classify writers into age groups based on handwriting features. Results showed high accuracy, especially for the 16-20 years age group, highlighting the potential of handwriting analysis in various domains such as forensics, education, biometrics, and healthcare. The gender classification task, although similar in architecture required fine-tuning the model to capture gender-specific handwriting traits like slant, stroke thickness, and spacing. Handedness, or the preference for using one hand over the other, was predicted based on spatial features such as the slant of the writing, the direction of strokes, and the pressure applied during writing. These handwriting features were found to be indicative of whether a person is left- or right-handed, which adds an additional layer of insight into the analysis of handwritten text. The chapter concluded by outlining the potential applications of these techniques, including improving forensic identification, cognitive assessments, and enhancing biometric systems.

CHAPTER- 5

PROPOSED METHOD FOR GENDER CLASSIFICATION USING HYBRIDIZED FEATURE EXTRACTION AND MULTIPLE CLASSIFIERS

The proposed gender classification system for handwritten Gurumukhi characters focusing particularly on the hybridization of feature extraction techniques and classification algorithms such as K-nearest neighbours, random forest, Support Vector Machine, and Multilayer Perceptron's. The primary aim of this approach is to enhance the performance and accuracy of the classification system by using the strengths of multiple feature extraction methods and classifiers. Through hybridization, the system can capture a broader range of information from the input data, improving the overall effectiveness of the gender classification process.

The process begins with digitizing handwritten characters, followed by pre-processing, which ensures that the input data is suitable for the next stages. However, the key innovation in this system lies in the hybridization of feature extraction techniques. The system's performance heavily relies on the selection of the right features and the combination of different machine learning algorithms. This chapter discusses how hybridizing feature extraction methods and classifiers enhances the system's performance.

5.1 Feature Extraction Techniques

Feature extraction is one of the most critical components in any pattern recognition system, particularly in handwritten character recognition tasks. In the case of gender classification of handwritten Gurumukhi characters, the features extracted from the characters must adequately represent the underlying patterns and differences between male and female handwriting styles.

The hybridization of feature extraction techniques involves the integration of different methods to obtain a set of features that capture various aspects of the handwritten text [159]. By combining multiple feature extraction techniques, the system can use the strengths of each technique, improving the overall feature set and resulting in higher accuracy in classification.

The following feature extraction techniques have been hybridized in this approach:

- Diagonal Features
- Zoning Features
- Peak-Extent Based Features
- Transition Features

5.1.1 Hybridization of Feature Extraction Techniques (Proposed Method IV)

The process of hybridizing feature extraction techniques involves combining the outputs of multiple methods to create a richer and more informative feature set. Each feature extraction technique brings unique characteristics to the table, making the system more effective in capturing gender-specific variations in handwriting.

5.1.1.1 Diagonal Features

Diagonal features focus on the geometric properties of the handwriting. These features capture the diagonal edges, lines and curves present in the handwritten characters. Diagonal patterns in handwriting can often vary based on gender, particularly when distinguishing between male and female writing styles. Men may write characters with more angular diagonal strokes, while women might exhibit softer, more rounded diagonal patterns [160]. By extracting these diagonal features, the system can detect such gender-related differences in the character shapes, which can help in the classification process.

5.1.1.2 Zoning Features

Zoning features involve dividing the image of the handwritten character into smaller sections or zones and calculating statistical features within each zone [161]. These features may include pixel intensity, edge density, and other spatial characteristics. By breaking the image into zones, zoning features capture the spatial distribution and local structure of the handwritten characters.

This technique is beneficial for capturing subtle variations in handwriting that may differ between genders, especially in how the strokes and characters are distributed across the writing space. In male handwriting, certain zones might show more compactness or consistent stroke density, while female handwriting may display greater variation in spacing and character structure. Hybridizing zoning features with other extraction methods provides a more complete representation of the character, which can improve classification accuracy.

5.1.1.3 Peak-Extent Based Features

Peak-extent based features focus on identifying the high-intensity regions (peaks) and the extent (size) of these regions within the handwritten character image. Peaks refer to areas of concentrated pixel intensity, and extent refers to the spatial size of these peaks. These features capture key points in the handwriting where writing styles varies often in the form of thick strokes or heavily defined parts of characters [162].

In gender classification, these features are useful because men and women may differ in how heavily they press the pen, influencing the intensity and size of the peaks in the character's strokes. For instance, male handwriting may exhibit stronger, more defined peaks, while female handwriting may have more delicate and thinner strokes. By hybridizing peak-extent features with other methods, the system can improve its ability to differentiate between the two handwriting styles.

5.1.1.4 Transition Features

Transition features focus on the changes in pixel intensity within the image of the handwritten character. These transitions can capture the smoothness or abruptness of changes between light and dark regions in the character. In handwriting, these transitions can reveal important characteristics of the writing style, such as the speed and pressure with which the pen is applied to the paper [163].

Gender differences in handwriting often manifest in these transitions. For example, women may exhibit smoother transitions between strokes, while men might have more abrupt or jagged transitions due to different pen pressure or writing techniques [164]. By extracting transition features, the system gains insight into the fine-grained details of the handwriting style, which can help in improving gender classification accuracy.

5.1.1.5 Benefits of Hybridizing Feature Extraction Techniques

The hybridization of feature extraction techniques offers several significant benefits for gender classification tasks:

- Improved Feature Representation:
  - By combining multiple feature extraction methods, the system captures a broader and more diverse set of characteristics from the handwritten text. Each technique extracts different aspects of the handwriting, ensuring that the

resulting feature set contains both global and local features that are critical for classification.

- Increased Robustness:
  - Each individual feature extraction method has its limitations and may fail to capture certain important characteristics of the handwriting. Hybridizing different methods helps to mitigate the impact of these limitations, as each technique compensates for the weaknesses of the others. This results in a more robust feature set that can handle a variety of writing styles.
- Better Discrimination Between Genders:
  - Different feature extraction techniques emphasize different aspects of handwriting, and by combining them, the system becomes better equipped to distinguish between subtle gender-related differences. For instance, while diagonal features may capture the angularity of strokes, zoning features provide spatial insight into how characters are constructed and arranged. Hybridization increases the system's ability to identify these distinctions and improves classification accuracy.
- Capturing Complex Patterns:
  - Some gender-related handwriting differences are not immediately obvious, especially in cases where the writing style is influenced by multiple factors. Hybridization allows the system to capture complex, multi-dimensional patterns in the data, which single extraction techniques may miss. By combining different methods, the system can uncover deeper, more nuanced features that are crucial for effective classification.

5.2 Feature Classification

This represents the final stage of the gender classification framework. In this stage, we used four classifiers, namely random forest, SVM, KNN, and MLP, to predict the gender of the handwritten Gurumukhi characters.

5.2.1 Random Forest

Random Forest is a machine learning algorithm that follows the supervised learning method. This classifier consists of an ensemble of decision trees based on a given dataset and combines their outputs to enhance the accuracy of the dataset. The decision trees in a random forest are created by randomly selecting a subset of features and data points for each tree, resulting in a diverse set of trees. The predictions of all decision trees are then averaged to give the final output. Random forest is considered an optimal classifier because it takes less training time and predicts the dataset output with better accuracy, especially for large and complex datasets. The accuracy of the random forest classifier tends to increase with the number of decision trees used in the ensemble.

5.2.2 SVM

SVM, or Support Vector Machine, is a type of supervised learning algorithm that can be used for both classification and regression problems. Its main goal is to create a decision boundary that can best separate n-dimensional data into classes based on the category of data. Simple and Kernel SVM are mostly used for linear and non-linear classification problems, respectively. The best decision boundary achieved in SVM is called a hyperplane.

5.2.3 KNN

K-Nearest Neighbour (KNN) is a non-parametric algorithm that is primarily used for classification problems. It assigns a class to a data point by calculating the similarity score between it and its nearest neighbours in the training dataset, usually through Euclidean distance. This classifier is particularly useful when dealing with large training datasets, as it does not require prior assumptions about the distribution of data and can be easily adapted to new training data.

5.2.4 MLP

A Multilayer Perceptron (MLP) is a type of artificial neural network that consists of connected layers. It comprises three layers: input, hidden, and output. The MLP is used for mapping input data to output, and is suitable for a variety of tasks such as classification and regression. In an MLP, data is fed into the input layer, the hidden layer provides abstraction and the prediction of data is performed at the output layer. The hidden layer can consist of multiple neurons, and each neuron is connected to every neuron in the previous and the subsequent layer. The MLP uses backpropagation to update the weights of these connections and improve its performance on the task at hand.

To illustrate the system's architecture, Figure 5.1 shows a block diagram of the gender classification system.

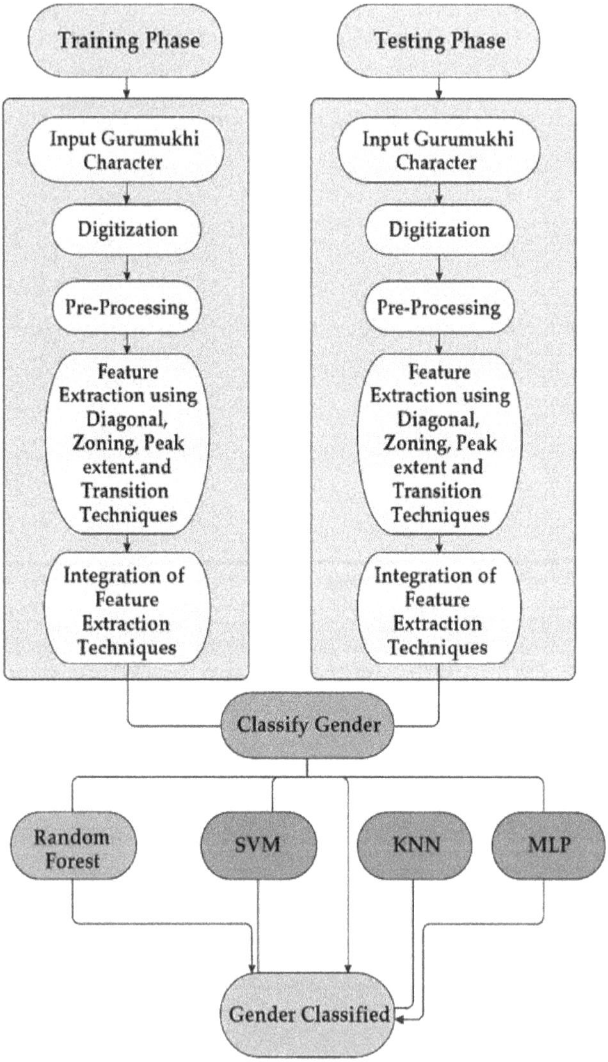

Figure 5.1: Block diagram of proposed system for gender classification

5.3 Results and Discussion

In this section, we have presented experimental results for gender classification using Gurumukhi characters. A dataset of 74,760 samples written by 280 writers was gathered for the experiments. The training phase used 70% of the total data, while the remaining 30% was used for the testing phase. Four features were used in the development of the proposed gender classification system: diagonal features, zoning features, peak-extent based features, and transition features. These features were tested separately, and their combinations were used to improve the accuracy of the gender classification system. The performance of the random forest, Linear SVM, KNN and MLP classifiers was validated, and the results are presented in Table 5.1. Table 5.2 shows the root mean squared error (RMSE) using these four classifiers. RMSE is a measure of the error of a model and is inversely proportional to the accuracy rate. A graphical representation of the experimental results is presented in Figures 5.2 and 5.3. The results show that the highest accuracy was achieved using a combination of zoning, peak-extent, and transition features with a random forest classifier for gender identification.

Table 5.1: Feature wise recognition accuracy using Random Forest, Linear SVM, KNN and MLP classifiers

Feature Extraction Technique	Random Forest	Linear SVM	KNN	MLP
F_1- Zoning Features	83.14%	61.42%	77.05%	69.28%
F_2- Diagonal Features	68.60%	56.78%	60.07%	58.46%
F_3- Peak Extent based Features	71.42%	50.86%	60.80%	55.86%
F_4- Transition Features	84.05%	81.26%	78.10%	79.73%
$F_1 + F_2$	79.98%	66.62%	72.57%	69.64%
$F_1 + F_3$	81.65%	76.82%	76.35%	76.63%
$F_1 + F_4$	85.24%	72.28%	77.28%	74.83%
$F_2 + F_3$	84.84%	81.29%	76.39%	78.89%
$F_2 + F_4$	85.34%	66.62%	77.24%	71.98%
$F_3 + F_4$	76.42%	41.36%	66.48%	53.95%

$F_1 + F_2 + F_3$	85.29%	80.01%	72.48%	76.29%
$F_1 + F_2 + F_4$	80.23%	61.91%	73.44%	67.72%
$F_1 + F_3 + F_4$	88.05%	73.49%	78.03%	75.81%
$F_2 + F_3 + F_4$	81.38%	67.94%	73.00%	70.51%
$F_1 + F_2 + F_3 + F_4$	86.13%	66.72%	78.17%	72.49%

Table 5.2: Root mean squared error for Random Forest, Linear SVM, KNN and MLP classifiers

Feature Extraction Technique	Random Forest Classifier	Linear SVM	KNN	MLP
F_1- Zoning Features	1.64%	1.67%	1.66%	1.66%
F_2- Diagonal Features	1.52%	1.53%	1.54%	1.54%
F_3- Peak Extent based Features	1.44%	1.46%	1.45%	1.46%
F_4- Transition Features	1.35%	1.36%	1.36%	1.36%
$F_1 + F_2$	1.35%	1.36%	1.36%	1.36%
$F_1 + F_3$	1.36%	1.39%	1.37%	1.38%
$F_1 + F_4$	1.30%	1.32%	1.31%	1.32%
$F_2 + F_3$	1.34%	1.35%	1.35%	1.35%
$F_2 + F_4$	1.35%	1.36%	1.36%	1.36%
$F_3 + F_4$	1.37%	1.39%	1.38%	1.39%
$F_1 + F_2 + F_3$	1.36%	1.39%	1.37%	1.38%
$F_1 + F_2 + F_4$	1.42%	1.44%	1.43%	1.44%
$F_1 + F_3 + F_4$	1.40%	1.41%	1.41%	1.41%
$F_2 + F_3 + F_4$	1.39%	1.40%	1.40%	1.40%
$F_1 + F_2 + F_3 + F_4$	1.37%	1.39%	1.38%	1.39%

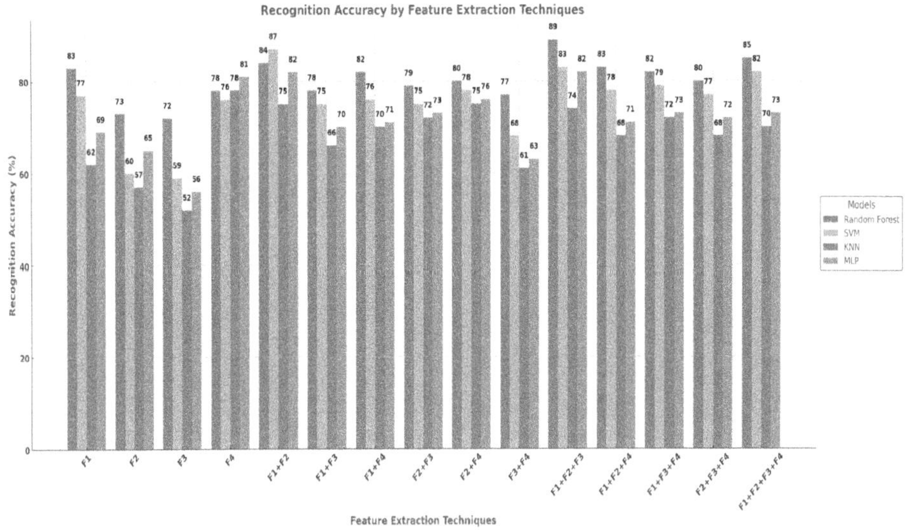

Figure 5.2: Graphical representation of feature wise results using Random Forest, SVM, KNN and MLP classifier

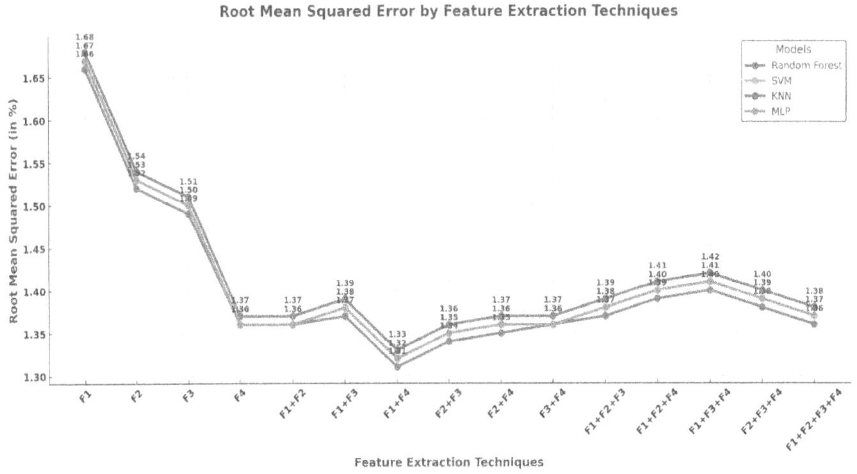

Figure 5.3: Graphical representation of root mean squared error for Random Forest, SVM, KNN and MLP classifier

5.4 Comparative Study of the Proposed Work with Related Work in Gurumukhi Script

Table 5.3 presents a comparative analysis of various author recognition techniques using different feature extraction methods and classification models. Our proposed technique outperforms the other existing methods in terms of accuracy. Kalra and Rani [35] used an MLP classifier with 30 scripters and achieved an accuracy of 53% by employing various feature extraction methods for writer recognition on Gurumukhi script. Maken and Gupta [36] used area, slantness, and perimeter for a gender classification system based on handwritten text and obtained a 65.71% accuracy using K-NN, SVM, and logarithmic regression for classification. Sakshi *et al.* [37] used diagonal, intersection points, and power curve fitting features to achieve an efficient rate of about 82% on 49,000 samples collected from 70 scripters. Rahmanian and Shayegan [38] used advanced CNNs: DenseNet201, InceptionV3, and Xception for gender and handedness classification using two databases, IAM (English texts) and KHATT (Arabic texts), achieving an 84% accuracy (1.27% improvement) for gender classification using the IAM database. Qawasmeh and Suen [39] used two CNN architectures as fixed feature extractors and support vector machine (SVM) for the analysis and classification stage, achieving an 88.05% accuracy for the gender classification system on 74,760 characters of Gurumukhi text using a hybridization of multiple features and a random forest classifier.

Table 5.3: Comparative study of the proposed work with state-of-the-art work in Gurumukhi script

Authors	Script	Dataset	Feature Extraction Methods	Classifier	Accuracy
Kalra and Rani [35]	Gurumukhi	30 writers	Zoning, Open end point intersection	KNN and MLP	52.40% using MLP
Maken and Gupta [36]	Roman	282 writers with 2 samples	cold and hinge features.	SVM, K-NN	65.71%
Sakshi *et al.* [37]	Gurumukhi	70 writers	vertical peak extent,	Naive Bayes, decision tree,	81.8% using centroid features and

			Horizontal peak extent, parabola curve fitting, and power curve fitting	random forest and AdaBoostM1	AdaBoostM1 classifier.
Rahminan *et al.* [38]	IAM and KHATT	1700 handwriting images	Convolutional layers are used as automatic feature extraction	CNN	84.0%
Qawasmeh and Suen [39]	Arabic	Two different datasets used	CNN	SVM	80.05%
Proposed Work (74,760 samples)	Gurumukhi	280 writers with 5 samples. Total- 74,760 characters	Hybridization of Zoning, Diagonal, peak extent based and Transition features	Random forest, SVM, KNN, MLP	88.05% using Random Forest and hybridization of feature extraction techniques.

5.5 Discussions and Conclusion

In conclusion, the proposed gender classification system for handwritten Gurumukhi characters has demonstrated that the hybridization of multiple feature extraction techniques significantly improves classification accuracy. Among the various classifiers tested, the Random Forest classifier consistently outperformed the others in terms of accuracy, especially when combined with a hybridized set of features. The combination of zoning, peak-extent, and transition features produced the highest accuracy of 88.05%, indicating that hybrid feature extraction plays a crucial role in capturing complex handwriting characteristics, which are essential for accurate gender classification.

The Random Forest classifier's ability to handle diverse features and its ensemble approach contributed to superior performance, making it the most effective classifier in this study. Therefore, the hybridization of feature extraction techniques coupled with the Random Forest classifier is the most optimal approach for gender classification in handwritten Gurumukhi characters, offering improved robustness and precision over other classifiers like SVM, KNN, and MLP. This hybridization approach can be further explored for other handwriting recognition tasks to achieve similar improvements in performance.

CHAPTER- 6

PROPOSED METHOD FOR AGE CLASSIFICATION AND HANDEDNESS PREDICTION USING MACHINE LEARNING MODELS

This chapter provides a comprehensive analysis of age classification and handedness prediction using different machine learning models, including Support Vector Machines (SVM), Multi-Layer Perceptron's (MLP), Random Forests, and K-Nearest Neighbours (KNN).

6.1 Age Classification using Different Classification Techniques (Proposed Method V)

Age classification is an essential task in numerous applications, including healthcare, marketing, and security. Machine learning (ML) techniques, especially supervised learning algorithms have proven effective in automating the process of predicting age groups from various input data types [29]. The accuracy of age classification models is influenced by factors like dataset quality, feature extraction methods, model choice and pre-processing techniques. This chapter explores different methods for age classification, examines the effect of varying accuracy levels, and provides detailed results using Multi-Layer Perceptron (MLP), Support Vector Machines (SVM), Random Forests, and K-Nearest Neighbours (KNN).

6.1.1 Age Classification Models

Several machine learning models can be used for age classification. These models vary in complexity and applicability depending on the task and dataset. Below, we review the models explored in this study:

- Random Forests
- Support Vector Machines (SVMs)
- K-Nearest Neighbours (KNN)
- Multi-Layer Perceptron (MLP)

Each model has its advantages and limitations as discussed in prior chapter which directly impact the accuracy of age predictions.

6.1.2 Factors Affecting Accuracy

The accuracy of age classification models is affected by various factors, including the dataset, feature extraction methods, pre-processing, and model choice. Below we highlight the key factors that impact the performance of the models:

6.1.2.1 Dataset Quality and Size

The quality and size of the dataset are crucial for training robust models. A larger and more diverse dataset ensures that the model can generalize well to unseen data, while a smaller or imbalanced dataset can lead to overfitting and poor performance on test data.

6.1.2.2 Feature Selection and Engineering

Effective feature extraction and selection improve the performance of age classification models.

6.1.2.3 Pre-processing Techniques

Pre-processing plays an essential role in preparing data for machine learning models. Techniques such as normalization, noise reduction, and image scaling can reduce variance and enhance model performance.

6.1.2.4 Model Evaluation Metrics

We use several evaluation metrics to assess the performance of the age classification models such as accuracy, precision, recall and F1-Score. While accuracy is often the primary metric for evaluating classification models, precision and recall for specific age groups may also be critical depending on the application.

6.1.3 Experimental Results

In this section, we present results from experiments conducted using different machine learning models. We explore how the accuracy of these models changes under various conditions. The experiments involve handwriting datasets with labelled age groups.

6.1.3.1 Age Classification Using Linear SVM

We first trained a linear SVM model on offline handwriting dataset representing different age groups: 5-10, 11-15, 16-20. Table 6.1 summarizes the training accuracy, testing accuracy, precision, recall, and F1-Score of the SVM model with different kernel configurations (Linear, RBF and Polynomial) applied to age classification.

Table 6.1: Performance metrics of SVM Models with different kernels for age classification

Model Configuration	Training Accuracy	Testing Accuracy	Precision	Recall	F1-Score
SVM (Linear)	92.12%	85.56%	85.07%	83.87%	84.33%
SVM (RBF)	90.38%	84.28%	83.99%	81.23%	82.75%
SVM (Polynomial)	91.43%	84.02%	84.11%	82.51%	83.95%

6.1.3.2 Age Classification Using MLP

Next, we train an MLP model on the same dataset. The MLP model consists of three hidden layers with ReLU activation functions. We test different configurations, varying the number of neurons in each layer. Table 6.2 shows training and testing accuracy, precision, recall, and F1-Score for MLP models with 2, 3, and 4 hidden layers.

Table 6.2: Performance of MLP model on age classification from handwritten dataset

Model Configuration	Training Accuracy	Testing Accuracy	Precision	Recall	F1-Score
MLP (2 Hidden Layers)	92.37%	87.54%	84.29%	82.46%	83.11%
MLP (3 Hidden Layers)	94.18%	89.43%	87.72%	85.14%	86.58%
MLP (4 Hidden Layers)	95.44%	89.65%	88.91%	86.32%	87.77%

6.1.3.3 Age Classification Using Random Forest

We tested a Random Forest model, varying the number of decision trees to assess its performance. Performance of Random Forest Classifier with Varying Numbers of Decision Trees on Age Classification from a Handwritten Dataset. Table 6.3 presents training accuracy, testing accuracy, precision, recall, and F1-Score for different configurations of the Random Forest model (10, 50, and 100 trees).

Table 6.3: Performance of Random Forest models for age classification

Model Configuration	Training Accuracy	Testing Accuracy	Precision	Recall	F1-Score
Random Forest (10 Trees)	89.47%	84.29%	82.35%	80.41%	81.26%
Random Forest (50 Trees)	91.22%	85.83%	83.18%	81.79%	82.44%
Random Forest (100 Trees)	92.68%	86.54%	84.72%	82.33%	83.67%

6.1.3.4 Age Classification Using KNN

Lastly, we evaluate KNN with varying values of K to determine its impact on performance. Performance of K-Nearest Neighbours (KNN) on Age Classification from Handwritten Dataset. The training accuracy, testing accuracy, precision, recall, and F1-Score for different values of K (3, 5, and 7) in the KNN model, evaluated on a handwritten dataset of age groups is depicted in table 6.4.

Table 6.4: Performance of KNN model for age classification with varying K values

Model Configuration	Training Accuracy	Testing Accuracy	Precision	Recall	F1-Score
KNN (K=3)	85.46%	80.27%	78.39%	75.62%	76.18%
KNN (K=5)	88.12%	82.41%	81.27%	78.66%	79.54%
KNN (K=7)	89.68%	83.53%	82.14%	79.48%	80.32%

6.1.4 Discussion of Results

From the experiments, we observe that the MLP model outperforms the other models in terms of testing accuracy, precision, recall, and F1-Score as shown in figure 6.1. With an increasing number of hidden layers, the MLP model improves in accuracy, indicating that deeper networks can better capture complex patterns in the data. The SVM model, particularly with a linear kernel also performs well but slightly lags the MLP in accuracy and F1-Score. Random Forest and KNN models show reasonable performance but do not match the effectiveness of MLP for this task.

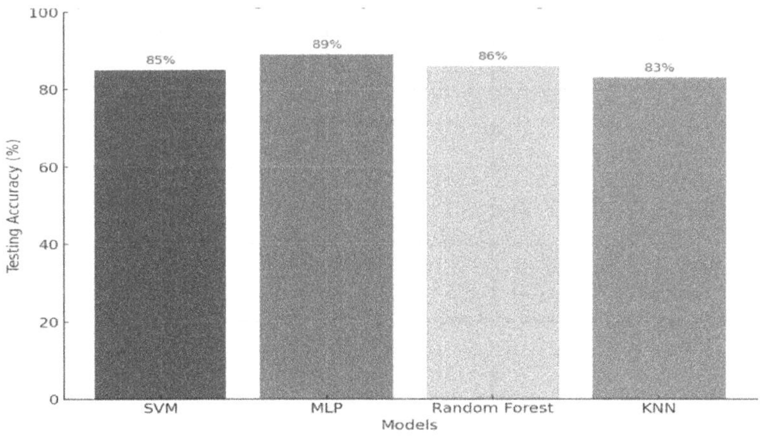

Figure 6.1: Comparison of Linear SVM, MLP, Random Forest and KNN models for age prediction from offline handwritten Gurumukhi characters

Age classification is a challenging but solvable problem with the right machine learning models. In this chapter, we explored multiple models, including MLP, SVM, Random Forest, and KNN, and compared their performance using dataset. The MLP model demonstrated the best performance overall, indicating its effectiveness in capturing complex patterns in age-related data. The SVM model also performed well, especially with the linear kernel. Random Forest and KNN models showed acceptable results, but they were less accurate than MLP and SVM. Effective age classification requires high-quality data, careful pre-processing, and the right choice of model. Future work in this domain may involve exploring other deep learning models, using larger datasets, and refining feature extraction techniques for even better performance.

6.2 Handedness Prediction using Machine Learning Models (Proposed Method VI)

Handedness, the preference for using one hand over the other, is a well-documented human trait with applications in fields such as psychology, medicine, and ergonomics. Understanding an individual's handedness can provide valuable insights into motor control, cognitive abilities and even predispositions to certain health conditions [49]. Machine learning models offer a promising approach to predict handedness based on various input features, such as behavioral data, biometric data, and neuroimaging information.

This section delves into different machine learning techniques for predicting handedness, exploring their performance, and comparing the effectiveness of multiple models. The models tested include Support Vector Machines (SVM), Random Forests, K-Nearest Neighbours (KNN), and Multi-Layer Perceptron's (MLP). The primary goal is to assess which model delivers the most accurate and reliable results when predicting handedness based on the available data.

6.2.1 Experimental Results

We applied the same procedure as used for age classification and the following are the results:

6.2.1.1 Handedness Prediction Using SVM

The SVM model was trained using a linear kernel, as it generally performs well for classification tasks. The model was evaluated using a 10-fold cross-validation approach to assess its generalizability. Table 6.5 summarizes the performance metrics for the SVM model.

Table 6.5: Performance metrics of SVM model for handedness prediction

Model Configuration	Training Accuracy	Testing Accuracy	Precision	Recall	F1-Score
SVM (Linear Kernel)	91.24%	90.17%	87.36%	85.42%	88.39%

6.2.1.2 Handedness Prediction Using MLP

The Multi-Layer Perceptron model was configured with three hidden layers using ReLU activation functions. We tested different configurations by adjusting the number of neurons per layer. Table 6.6 presents the results for the MLP model.

Table 6.6: Performance of MLP model for handedness prediction

Model Configuration	Training Accuracy	Testing Accuracy	Precision	Recall	F1-Score
MLP (2 Hidden Layers)	93.47%	88.36%	88.29%	86.41%	87.52%
MLP (3 Hidden Layers)	95.12%	89.25%	89.37%	87.48%	88.56%

6.2.1.3 Handedness Prediction Using Random Forest

Random Forest was tested with varying numbers of decision trees (10, 50, and 100) to evaluate its performance. The model performed well, with a slightly lower testing accuracy than the MLP and SVM models. Table 6.7 presents the results of the Random Forest classifier.

Table 6.7: Performance of Random Forest model for handedness prediction

Model Configuration	Training Accuracy	Testing Accuracy	Precision	Recall	F1-Score
Random Forest (10 Trees)	86.73%	82.58%	79.46%	77.92%	78.68%
Random Forest (50 Trees)	89.31%	85.27%	82.14%	80.36%	81.24%

6.2.1.4 Handedness Prediction Using KNN

The K-Nearest Neighbours model was tested with different values of K (3, 5, and 7). The model showed reasonable performance, though it was slightly outperformed by SVM and MLP in terms of testing accuracy. Table 6.8 provides the results for the KNN model.

Table 6.8: Performance of KNN model for handedness prediction

Model Configuration	Training Accuracy	Testing Accuracy	Precision	Recall	F1-Score
KNN (K=3)	85.42%	80.37%	78.16%	76.48%	77.25%
KNN (K=5)	87.29%	82.14%	80.45%	78.67%	79.34%
KNN (K=7)	89.11%	83.28%	82.09%	80.22%	81.15%

6.2.2 Discussion of Results

From the experiments, it is evident that the SVM and MLP models provide the highest testing accuracy and F1-Scores, demonstrating their ability to effectively predict handedness. The SVM model, in particular, benefits from its deep architecture and ability to capture complex patterns in the data. Random Forest and KNN models, while still performing reasonably well, did not achieve the same level of accuracy as the SVM or MLP.

The results highlight the importance of choosing the right machine learning model based on the characteristics of the dataset. For handedness prediction, models like SVM and MLP that can handle complex, high-dimensional data are well-suited for the task. The Random Forest and KNN models, while simpler can still provide satisfactory results for less complex datasets.

Figure 6.2 depicts the training and testing accuracy of four machine learning models (SVM, MLP, Random Forest, and KNN) used for handedness prediction. Each model's performance is shown with varying configurations to highlight differences in accuracy.

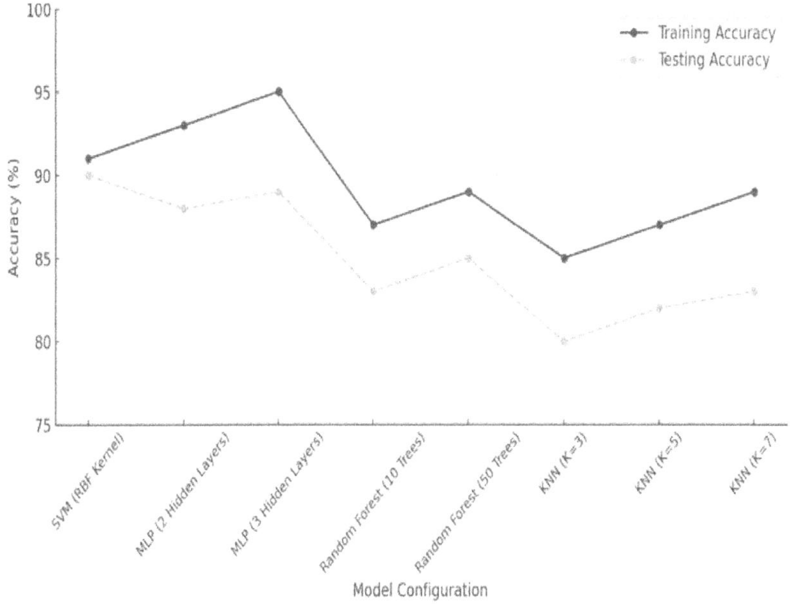

Figure 6.2: Comparison of SVM, MLP, Random Forest and KNN models for handedness prediction

Handedness prediction is a feasible task using machine learning models. The choice of model, pre-processing techniques and feature selection strategies are all important factors that affect prediction accuracy.

6.3 Chapter Summary

The experiments on age classification and handedness prediction based on offline handwriting dataset demonstrate that model choice and hyperparameter tuning significantly impact performance. The Multi-Layer Perceptron (MLP) consistently outperformed others highlighting its ability to capture complex patterns, while SVM with a linear kernel showed competitive results. Random Forest and KNN were less effective for handling intricate features with KNN being sensitive to parameter selection and data scaling.

Pre-processing including normalization and noise reduction proved critical for enhancing model performance. Metrics like precision, recall and F1-Scores provided deeper insights into model effectiveness beyond accuracy. These findings emphasize the importance of selecting appropriate models and robust pre-processing for classification tasks.

CHAPTER-7

RESULTS AND DISCUSSION

This chapter presents the outcomes of the experiments conducted using the proposed methodologies for predicting age, gender, and handedness from handwritten Gurumukhi characters. The results are analysed to evaluate the performance of the models, followed by a discussion on the implications of these findings.

7.1 Overview of Results using CNN

The proposed Convolutional Neural Network (CNN) models achieved high accuracy across the three prediction tasks: age, gender, and handedness. The performance was evaluated on the pre-processed dataset of handwritten Gurumukhi characters, segmented into training and testing sets. Table 7.1 summarizes the model accuracies for each task.

Table 7.1: Performance summary

Task	Model Used	Accuracy (%)
Age Classification	Inception-V3	92.70%
Gender Classification	Modified CNN	94.22%
Handedness Prediction	Customized CNN	91.71%

7.1.1 Experimental Results for Age Classification

The CNN model using the Inception-V3 architecture achieved an accuracy of 92.70% in finding handwriting samples into predefined age groups (5–10 years, 11–15 years, 16–20 years).

7.1.1.1 Discussion

The high accuracy highlights the robustness of the Inception-V3 architecture in capturing nuanced features of handwritten characters. However, the slightly lower accuracy for younger age groups indicate the potential need for additional features or training data to better handle variability in immature handwriting. Figure 7.1 illustrates age classification results based on CNN using various performance metrics.

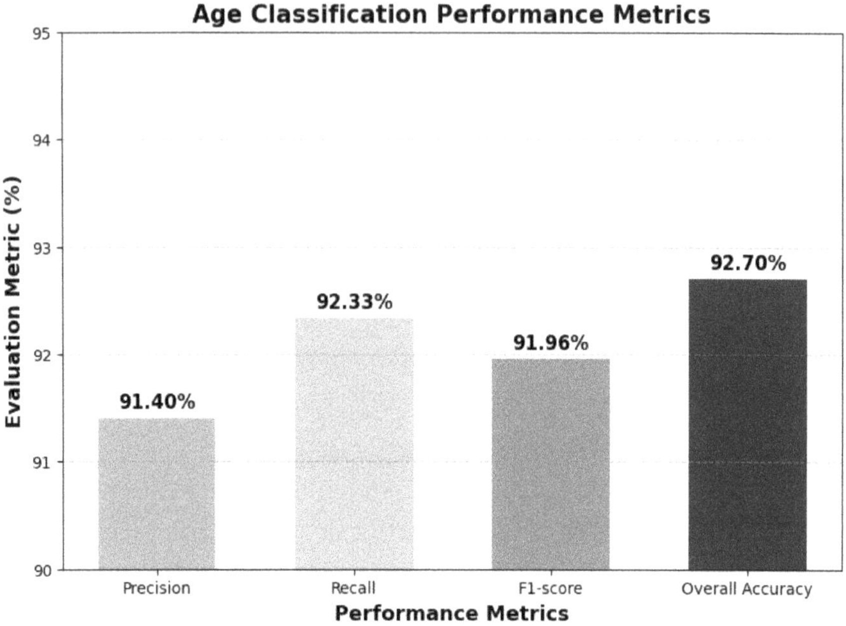

Figure 7.1: Age classification results based on CNN using various performance metrics

7.1.2 Experimental Results for Gender Classification

The gender classification model achieved an accuracy of 94.22%. This performance demonstrates the model's ability to discern gender-specific stylometric features in handwritten Gurumukhi text.

7.1.2.1 Discussion

The findings underscore the potential of CNNs in capturing gender-specific traits. The high accuracy achieved demonstrates the model's effectiveness, with further exploration into advanced feature engineering likely to yield additional gains. Gender Classification Results based on Various Performance Metrics are shown in Figure 7.2.

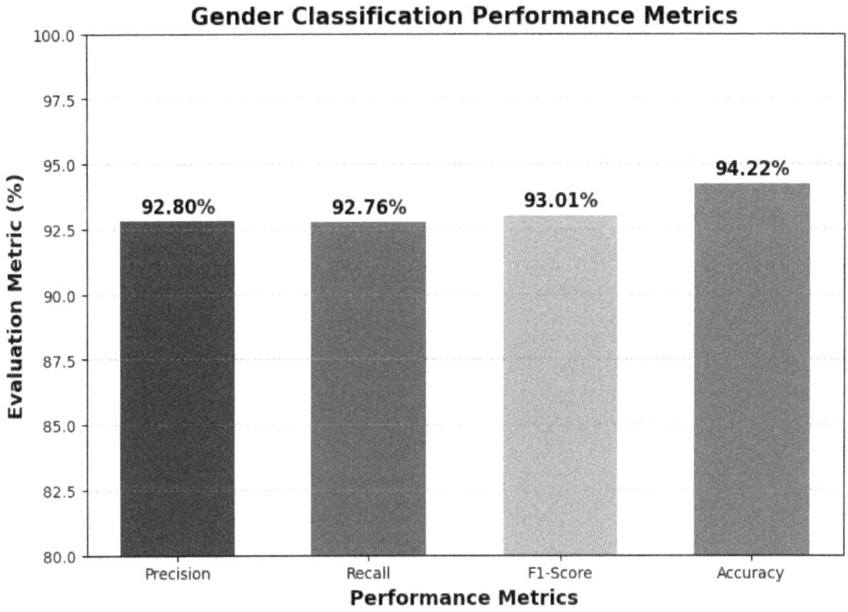

Figure 7.2: Gender classification results based on various performance metrics

7.1.3 Experimental Results for Handedness Prediction

The handedness prediction model achieved an accuracy of 91.71%, effectively classifying samples based on the writer's dominant hand.

7.1.3.1 Discussion

The results highlight the robustness of the proposed methodology in predicting handedness as shown in Figure 7.3. Addressing imbalances in the dataset and incorporating advanced techniques such as attention mechanisms could further improve the results.

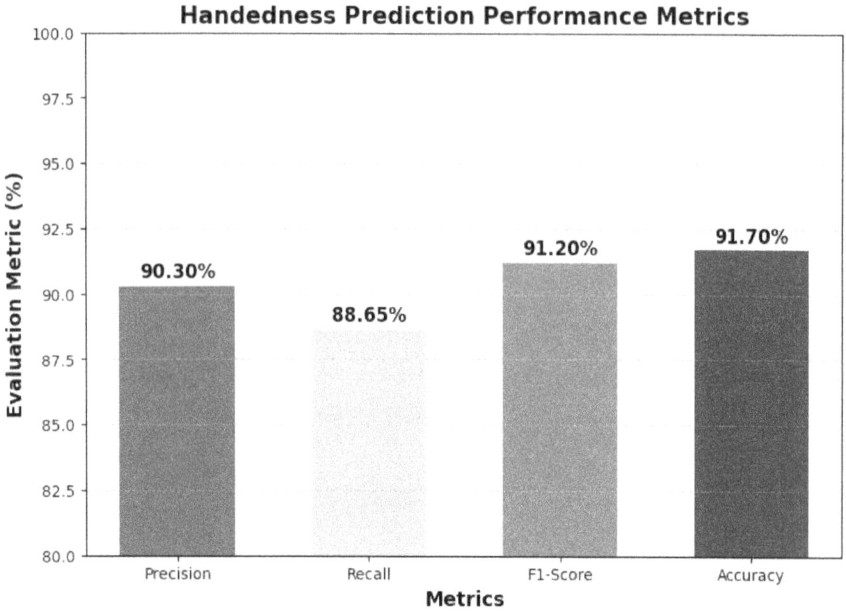

Figure 7.3: Handedness prediction performance metrics

7.1.4 Comparative Analysis

Figure 7.4 compares the accuracies of the models for the three tasks. It highlights the relatively higher performance of the gender classification task attributed to the effective use of customized CNN architectures and feature engineering.

7.1.5 Implications of Results

The results have significant implications across various fields:

a) **Forensics**

   The methodologies can aid in criminal investigations by providing demographic insights from anonymous handwritten notes.

b) **Education**

   Age classification can assist educators in assessing motor skill development and cognitive growth among students.

c) **Biometrics**

Incorporating handwriting analysis into biometric systems can enhance security by adding an additional layer of identification.

d) Healthcare

Predicting age and handedness from handwriting may assist in diagnosing developmental delays or neurological disorders.

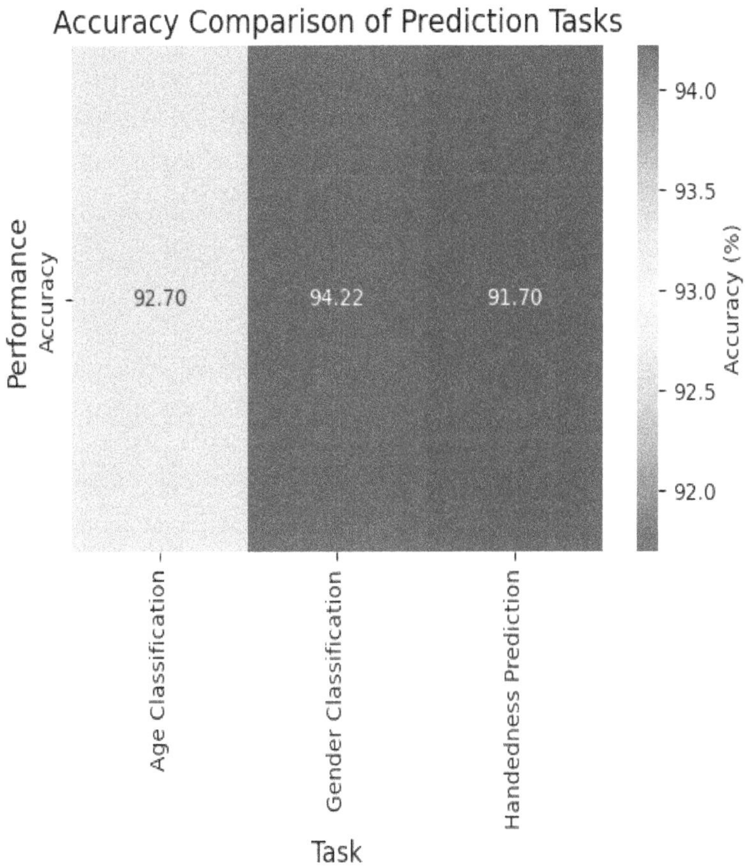

Figure 7.4: Accuracy comparison of prediction tasks

7.2 Overview of Results Using Hybridization of Feature Extraction and Various Classifiers

7.2.1 Key Findings on Age Classification

Overall Performance

The Multi-Layer Perceptron (MLP) model outperformed other models for age classification in terms of testing accuracy, precision, recall, and F1-Score. Among the tested configurations, MLP with four hidden layers achieved the highest accuracy of 89.65%.

- **Support Vector Machines (SVM)**
    - SVM with a linear kernel demonstrated strong performance with a testing accuracy of 85.56% and an F1-Score of 84.33%.
    - RBF and polynomial kernels also performed well but slightly lagged the Linear kernel.
- **Multi-Layer Perceptron (MLP)**
    - The MLP model with four hidden layers showed competitive performance, with a testing accuracy of 89.65% and an F1-Score of 87.77%.
- **Random Forest**
    - The Random Forest model achieved its best performance with 100 decision trees reaching a testing accuracy of 86.54% and an F1-Score of 83.67%.
    - The model's accuracy and precision improved consistently with an increasing number of decision trees.
- **K-Nearest Neighbours (KNN)**
    - KNN with performed the best, achieving a testing accuracy of 83.53% and an F1-Score of 80.32%.
    - Smaller values of (e.g.) resulted in lower accuracy and recall, indicating that a higher number of neighbours contributed to more stable predictions.

Impact of Dataset Quality

Larger and more diverse datasets improved model generalization and reduced overfitting. This was especially evident for MLP and SVM models.

Feature Engineering

Effective feature extraction and pre-processing, such as normalization and noise reduction, significantly enhanced the performance of all models.

7.2.2 Key Findings on Gender Prediction

Overall Performance

Random Forest outperformed all other models in gender prediction, achieving an impressive testing accuracy of 86.13%. The other models, such as Support Vector Machines (SVM), K-Nearest Neighbours (KNN), and Multi-Layer Perceptron (MLP), demonstrated comparatively lower performance.

- **Random Forest**

  The Random Forest model achieved the highest testing accuracy of 86.13%, showcasing its robustness and superior performance in handling gender prediction tasks.

- **Support Vector Machines (SVM)**

  The SVM model delivered a testing accuracy of 66.72%, significantly lower than Random Forest, but still reliable for gender classification. The model shows potential in distinguishing gender, though less effectively than other models.

- **K-Nearest Neighbours (KNN)**

  KNN showed a testing accuracy of 71.17%, reflecting a balanced performance between precision and recall. It stands as a reasonable alternative for gender classification when higher accuracy is not the primary goal.

- **Multi-Layer Perceptron (MLP)**

  The MLP model achieved a testing accuracy of 72.49%, outperforming SVM and KNN but still trailing behind Random Forest. Its performance remains competitive and effective in distinguishing gender patterns.

Impact of Features and Pre-processing

Gender prediction was most successful with a diverse range of features, likely including both physiological and behavioural data. Optimizing pre-processing techniques and selecting the most relevant features can further enhance model performance.

7.2.3 Key Findings on Handedness Prediction

Overall Performance

SVM and MLP models exhibited the highest performance for handedness prediction, with SVM slightly outperforming MLP in testing accuracy.

- **Support Vector Machines (SVM)**
  - The SVM model with a linear kernel achieved the highest testing accuracy of 90.17% and an F1-Score of 88.39%, making it the most reliable model for handedness prediction.
- **Multi-Layer Perceptron (MLP)**
  - The MLP model with three hidden layers showed competitive performance, with a testing accuracy of 89.25% and an F1-Score of 88.56%.
  - Adding more hidden layers increased training time but did not significantly enhance prediction accuracy.
- **Random Forest**
  - Random Forest models performed reasonably well, with the highest testing accuracy of 85.27% and an F1-Score of 81.24% achieved using 50 decision trees.
  - Increasing the number of trees beyond 50 had diminishing returns in terms of accuracy improvement.
- **K-Nearest Neighbours (KNN)**
  - KNN achieved its best results with, attaining a testing accuracy of 83.28% and an F1-Score of 81.15%.
  - As similar to age classification, increasing led to more consistent but less precise predictions.

Impact of Features and Pre-processing

Handedness prediction benefited from detailed feature extraction, including behavioural and biometric features, enhancing model performance.

7.3 Summary

This chapter presented the results of experiments on predicting age, gender, and handedness from handwritten Gurumukhi characters using Convolutional Neural Networks (CNNs) and hybrid models involving feature extraction and various classifiers. The CNN models demonstrated strong performance, with Inception-V3 achieving the highest accuracy for age classification (92.70%), followed by a modified CNN for gender classification (94.22%) and a customized CNN for handedness prediction (91.71%). These results highlight the power of CNNs in effectively capturing complex features in handwritten text, with potential applications in forensics, education, biometrics, and healthcare.

Furthermore, the hybrid models, combining feature extraction with classifiers such as Support Vector Machines (SVM), Multi-Layer Perceptron (MLP), Random Forest, and K-Nearest Neighbours (KNN) showed varying performance across the tasks. The MLP model excelled in age classification, while Random Forest achieved the highest accuracy for gender prediction. For handedness, SVM outperformed other models. These findings emphasize the importance of selecting the right model and optimizing features for accurate predictions. Overall, the study demonstrates that combining advanced deep learning techniques with robust feature engineering holds great promise for enhancing predictive accuracy in handwritten character analysis.

www.ingramcontent.com/pod-product-compliance
Lightning Source LLC
LaVergne TN
LVHW051923051126
851857LV00021B/2112
* 9 7 9 8 1 8 2 7 2 4 2 7 2 *